SHIPPING

ON THE THAMES AND THE PORT OF LONDON

DURING THE 1940s–1980s

The PLA former headquarters building at Tower Hill, known as the 'Wedding Cake', opened in 1922. It was sold to an insurance firm in June 1972 as it was too large and expensive by this time of decline. *Photo by Malcolm Batten.*

The PLA Coat of arms on the Passenger Terminal at Tilbury – this translates as 'May the Port of the Empire flourish.'

SHIPPING
ON THE THAMES AND THE PORT OF LONDON
DURING THE 1940s–1980s

Malcolm Batten

PEN & SWORD
TRANSPORT
AN IMPRINT OF PEN & SWORD BOOKS LTD.
YORKSHIRE – PHILADELPHIA

First published in Great Britain in 2022 by
Pen and Sword Transport
An imprint of
Pen & Sword Books Ltd.
Yorkshire - Philadelphia

ISBN 978 1 39901 840 1

Typeset by SJmagic DESIGN SERVICES, India.

Printed and bound in India by Replika Press Pvt. Ltd.

Pen & Sword Books Ltd incorporates the imprints of Pen & Sword Books Archaeology, Atlas, Aviation, Battleground, Discovery, Family History, History, Maritime, Military, Naval, Politics, Railways, Select, Transport, True Crime, Fiction, Frontline Books, Leo Cooper, Praetorian Press, Seaforth Publishing, Wharncliffe and White Owl.

For a complete list of Pen & Sword titles please contact

PEN & SWORD BOOKS LIMITED
47 Church Street, Barnsley, South Yorkshire, S70 2AS, England
E-mail: enquiries@pen-and-sword.co.uk
Website: www.pen-and-sword.co.uk

or

PEN AND SWORD BOOKS
1950 Lawrence Rd, Havertown, PA 19083, USA
E-mail: Uspen-and-sword@casematepublishers.com
Website: www.penandswordbooks.com

FSC MIX Paper from responsible sources FSC® C016779

CONTENTS

INTRODUCTION

Reg Batten was born in 1914 and grew up in Canning Town in the heart of London's Dockland. His father was a boilermaker working in the docks; his grandfather was a merchant seaman, originally from Plymouth before moving to London. So perhaps it was inevitable that Reg would have an interest in shipping. As a boy, he regularly used to walk down to the Tidal Basin swing bridge to view the ships in the Royal Victoria Dock, or down to the Thames riverside to watch the seemingly never-ending stream of shipping, particularly the paddle steamers, the tugs hauling strings of lighters, and of course the magnificent Thames sailing barges, still commercially active in those days.

But he was not encouraged to follow the family tradition of a marine career. Instead, with an interest in railways and a talent for drawing he joined as a trainee draughtsman at Stratford Railway Works. However, he was thwarted when he failed a medical and instead made a career in the printing, and later photographic and insurance trades.

Reg started taking photographs in 1930. Railways and the countryside would always form the bulk of his photographic output, but he did take a few photos of the local shipping from time to time – possibly to use a film up before processing it.

It was not until 1976, when he was made redundant at the age of sixty-two as a result of his employers relocating out of London, that he rediscovered ship photography. By now the London Docks were in a state of transition. In order to cope with new shipping and distribution technology – containerisation, Roll-on, Roll-off ferries etc. the Port of London Authority had decided that from 1968 all new investment would be centred on Tilbury and that the older docks nearer to London would be closed down. Already the St Katharine Docks and London Docks had been closed in 1968. Further partial closures had followed in the East India and Surrey Commercial Docks. Meanwhile investment down-river had seen new berths opened in Tilbury Dock, including a specialised container-handling facility which opened in 1970.

Reg now began to regularly visit both Woolwich and the Royal Docks entrance at Gallions Reach, North Woolwich, where shipping for the Royals and the docks and wharves further upriver would pass. He also frequently travelled to Tilbury Riverside station, right by Tilbury Landing Stage where the ferry crossed to Gravesend, and alongside the Ocean Liner (now Cruise) terminal. Here he could photograph all the traffic for Tilbury Docks as well as that heading upriver toward London. Sometimes he would take the ferry to the Gravesend side, where the light was better for photography. He would continue these visits until 1983 when the Royal Docks, once the largest enclosed docks in the world, closed to all traffic.

These years, through the 1970s and early 1980s were a fascinating time for shipping enthusiasts and photographers. There was still plenty to see, but it was all in a process of transition. Traditional cargo ships and coasters were working alongside new purpose-built container ships and feeders, often carrying containers as deck cargo. Roll-on-Roll-off ships served purpose-built berths within Tilbury Dock. Tankers and dredgers berthed at various specialised terminals along the river. Colliers still brought coal to the remaining coal-fired power stations, although they were being phased out as a result of the Clean Air Act. Sludge boats disposed of sewage. There were short-lived experiments like the Lykes Line barge carriers. With many riverside wharves and warehouses still in use, there were numerous lighters with their attendant tugs to marshal them around. For ship-handling within the enclosed docks the PLA had their own tugs, while elsewhere ships were handled by those owned by London Tugs Ltd (Alexandra Towing Co. from 1975).

Passenger shipping was mostly centred on Tilbury, but there was an experimental hydrofoil service operated by P&O between London and Zeebrugge. The car ferries at Tilbury had given way to the Dartford Tunnel, opened in November 1963. But the passenger ferries remained, worked by British Rail Sealink to connect with the trains which still ran into Tilbury Riverside station at this time. The Woolwich ferry had been re-equipped with new diesel ferries in 1963. They were run by the Greater London Council which would later be abolished. But the ferries continued, initially worked by Greenwich Council, and have continued to this day, the 1963 built vessels being replaced in 2018.

Shipping came from all over the world. Many ships were still owned (and crewed) by British companies at this time. There were cargo ships from China, container ships from Australia, barge carriers from the USA, Russian timber ships, Scandinavian Ro-Ro ships, Dutch and German coasters and so forth. Ships from behind the Iron Curtain also included Russian and Polish cruise ships.

This book aims to capture some of the variety of shipping to be seen on the Thames during this period, when the old pattern of ships and ship-handling gave way to the systems more familiar today. There are also photographs from the classic days of the 1940s–1960s before the new technology started to appear. Most of these photographs have not previously appeared in print, but from the 1990s, I wrote several articles to accompany Reg's photographs, which were published in magazines such as *Old Glory* and *Vintage Spirit*. Some of these articles are reproduced in full or in part, updated, in this book.

Malcolm Batten, 2020.

All photos are by Reg Batten except where credited. Please note that the dates given for when they were taken are estimates, as he did not keep accurate notes.

Reg Batten (1914 - 2014)

ACKNOWLEDGEMENTS/ BIBLIOGRAPHY

Batten, Malcolm, *River Thames Shipping since 2000: Cargo shipping* (Stroud: Amberley, 2019)

Batten, Malcolm, *River Thames Shipping since 2000: Passenger ships, ferries, heritage shipping and more* (Stroud: Amberley, 2020)

Benham, Harvey, *Down Tops'l: The story of East Coast sailing barges, 2nd ed* (London: Harrap, 1971)

Brown, Paul, *Historic ships: the survivors* (Stroud: Amberley, 2010)

Chesterton, D. Ridley, *Coastal Ships* (Shepperton: Ian Allan, 1967)

Clegg, W. Paul, *Docks and Ports: 2, London* (Shepperton: Ian Allan, 1987)

Dunn, Laurence, *Laurence Dunn's Thames Shipping, Second edition* (Greenwich: Carmania Press, 1994)

Ellmers, Chris, & Werner, Alex, *Dockland Life: A pictorial history of London's Docks 1860–2000,* (Edinburgh: Mainstream, 2000)

Hallam, W. B., *Blow Five: A History of the Alexandra Towing Co. Ltd* (Liverpool: Journal of Commerce and Shipping Telegraph Ltd, 1976)

Lunn, Geoff, *Port of London shipping: An era of change* (Stroud: Tempus, 2004)

Lunn, Geoff, *Port of London through time* (Stroud: Amberley, 2011)

McCutcheon, Campbell, *Port of Tilbury in the 60s and 70s* (Stroud: Amberley, 2013)

McCutcheon, Campbell, *Thames Shipping in the 1960s and 1970s* (Stroud: Amberley, 2013)

McNeil, Ian, *Hydraulic power* (London: Longman, 1972)

Moody, Bert, *Ocean ships. Fifth edition* (Shepperton: Ian Allan, 1974)

Ormston, John M., *The Five Minute Crossing: The Tilbury–Gravesend Ferries* (Thurrock: Thurrock Local History Society, 1998)

The Port of London [directory] (London: Port of London Authority, 1963)

Williams, David L. & De Kerbrech, Richard, *Diesel tugs: a colour portfolio* (Hersham: Ian Allan, 2006)

Williams, David L., *Steam tugs: a colour portfolio* (Hersham: Ian Allan, 2002)

Wiltshire, Andrew, *Thames tugs in colour* (Portishead: Bernard McCall, 2017)

Special thanks to Dave Salisbury and Simon Olsen of the World Ship Society for tracking down information about many of the ships featured here.

Maps reproduced by courtesy of the Port of London Authority/Museum of London Docklands

THE PORT OF LONDON AUTHORITY

London's docks grew in a piecemeal pattern. Originally there were the 'Legal Quays' at Billingsgate where all imported goods had to be delivered for inspection and assessment by customs officers. By the end of the eighteenth century the riverbank around the Tower of London was crowded with wharves and warehouses, while the tidal river was congested with shipping trying to reach them. Smuggling and theft were rife. The solution was to build enclosed docks with a permanent water level controlled by lock gates. The first commercial dock to be opened, by the West India Dock Company in 1802, was on the Isle of Dogs. Four years later a second dock was added, and the East India Dock Company opened its own dock at Blackwall. Others followed, for example London Docks (1805), St Katharine Dock (1828), Poplar Dock (1852), all on the north bank; and what were to become known as the Surrey Commercial Docks were developed from around the Howlands Great Dock on the south side. This had been the first enclosed dock, constructed back in 1696, but was used only for fitting out, ship repair and by the whaling fleet.

Victoria (later Royal Victoria) Dock opened further down river in 1855. This was the first to be designed specifically for steamships and to have rail access. This was followed by Millwall Docks in 1868, Royal Albert Dock in 1880, and the first development at Tilbury, 22 nautical miles downriver in 1886.

By the end of the nineteenth century, London had already become the world's leading port. It handled more cargo by both weight and value than any other UK port. But the various docks were owned by a number of companies who competed not only with each other, but also with the private riverside wharves. They were losing money. The 'Free Water Clause' gave lightermen free access to the enclosed docks. It was estimated that by 1900 over 80 per cent of all imports handled in the enclosed docks was being discharged to lighters for onward carriage to private wharves, earning the dock companies no revenue on this cargo. Navigational facilities were also less than ideal. For instance, the Royal Albert Dock had an entrance lock with a depth of nearly 30ft, but the navigable channel in Gallions Reach approaching the lock was only 18ft deep. Other ports both in the UK and overseas were expanding faster and more efficiently.

A Royal Commission was set up in 1900 and published its findings in 1902. It recommended a single, unified public authority to run the docks, act in the interests of all port users and provide whatever navigational facilities were considered necessary. The government accepted the findings and placed a bill before Parliament in 1903. This finally became law on 21 December 1908, and thus the Port of London Authority came into being in 1909.

The PLA was made responsible for administering docks and shipping on the tidal Thames from the North Sea to Teddington Lock, a distance of 95 miles. Duties included provision of approach channels of adequate depth, providing barge and ship mooring points, licensing of riverside wharves which projected below the high-water mark into the water, wreck disposal, ship towage within the docks, and surveying. The PLA also took over the responsibilities of the Thames Conservancy Board. Duties that remained outside their remit were ship towage on the river (private towing companies), pilotage and lights (Trinity House), river police (The Metropolitan Police) and the Port Health Authority (City of London Corporation). The private wharves also remained with their owners and the 'Free Water Clause' remained intact.

The PLA was run by a board of some nominated and some elected members, representing various bodies with interests in the running of the port. It raised revenue by charges on shipping using the port, and on cargoes handled and stored in the port warehouses.

Most of the docks had already been built when the PLA was formed. However, in 1921 the 'Royal' group of docks was completed with the opening of the King George V (KGV) dock by His Majesty on 8 July. Between them, the Royal Docks comprised the largest area of impounded dock water in the world, with over 11 miles of quays. A dry dock 750ft long by 100ft wide was provided at King George V dock complementing two other dry docks in the Royal Albert Dock. The docks had rail connections to the main lines, the PLA having its own internal fleet of dock shunting locomotives until railway operations ceased in 1970.

Amongst other developments was the opening of the new passenger terminal at Tilbury in 1930, built in conjunction with the LMS railway who built a new station building alongside.

London's docks were to suffer severe damage in the blitz, especially on the night of 7 September 1940 when Surrey Commercial Docks lost nearly 250 acres of stored timber in the resulting blaze. But they recovered and were rebuilt during the 1950s, although imports now far exceeded exports.

The docks reached their highest point of activity in 1964 when trade exceeded 61 million tons, but change was soon to come. The introduction of new cargo handling methods with containerisation and Roll-on, Roll-off ferries made the old docks redundant as they were not suited to the quick turn-rounds of the new technologies, nor could some of them handle the larger ships being built. New facilities were developed at Tilbury and the older docks gradually closed. First to go were the East India Docks and the Regent's Canal Dock (which was operated by the British Waterways Board) in 1967. The small St Katharine Dock and London Docks closed in 1968. St Katharine Dock, the smallest, was redeveloped as a marina. Various preserved vessels were offered moorings there, and although most of these have since moved on, the dock is still home for a selection of the former Thames sailing barges.

The other London docks followed in the 1970s and 1980s – the Surrey Docks, Millwall and West India Docks. The PLA internal railway system also closed in 1970. Finally, the Royals closed commercially in 1981, although some ships remained laid up there until 1985. After that all activity was concentrated at Tilbury.

The scheduled passenger services had largely ended by the mid-1970s as had the boat trains that brought passengers to Tilbury. Where once immigrants, e.g. from the *Empire Windrush*, and emigrants ('£10 Poms') had passed through, cruise liner passengers were now the main focus and this would be recognised in 1989 when the Landing Stage was refurbished and renamed the London International Cruise Terminal.

The private wharves were also severely affected. Between September 1967 and January 1970, thirty-two riverside wharves closed, although some private container terminals opened, such as Victoria Deep Wharf at Greenwich in 1973.

The closed docks passed to the London Docklands Development Corporation who transformed the sites. The Millwall and West India Docks became Docklands – the business and housing developments around Canary Wharf. The Royals are now home to London City Airport, the University of East London and the Excel Exhibition Centre. Maritime access is still maintained to West India Dock – often used by vessels on courtesy visits, and to the Royals – used for events at Excel such as the former London International Boat Show.

The PLA is no longer a dock owner as Tilbury was sold off to a management buyout in 1992, and then four years later passed to Forth Ports Ltd. The PLA still retains many of its other functions however. London remains one of the top three UK ports, handling over 50 million tonnes of cargo each year. The tidal river Thames also attracts many leisure users, particularly in the upper reaches. The onetime PLA headquarters building near the Tower of London, which was opened in 1922, was sold off in 1972. It is now based at Gravesend in the building completed in 1959 to house the Thames Navigation Service.

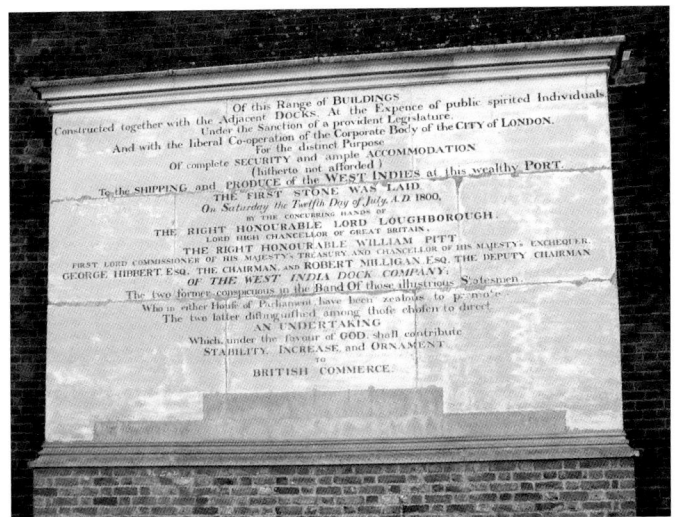

This plaque commemorates the commencement of construction of the West India Dock in 1800 – the first commercial enclosed dock in London. *Photo by Malcolm Batten.*

St Katharine and London Docks 1950s.

SURREY
COMMERCIAL
DOCKS

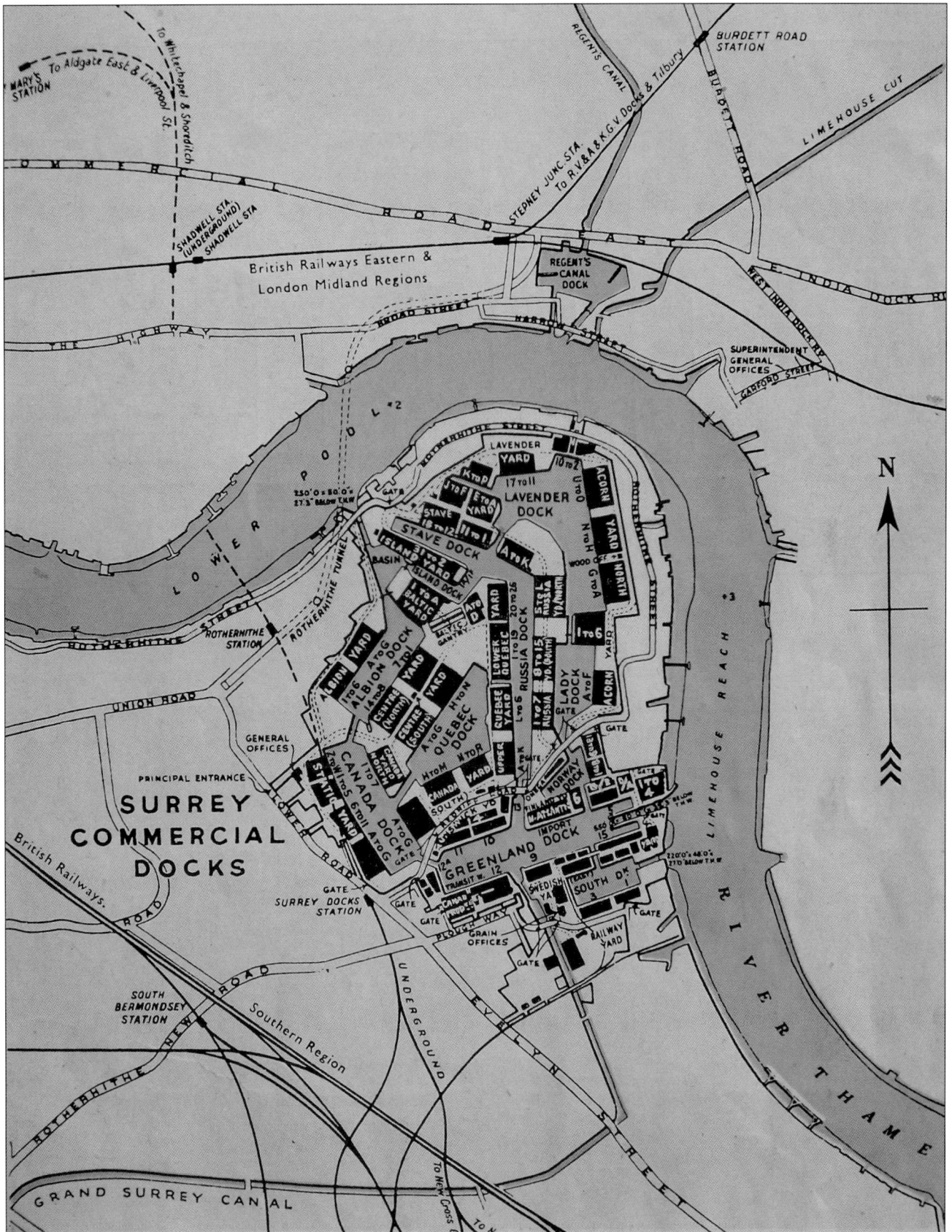

Surrey Commercial Docks 1950s.

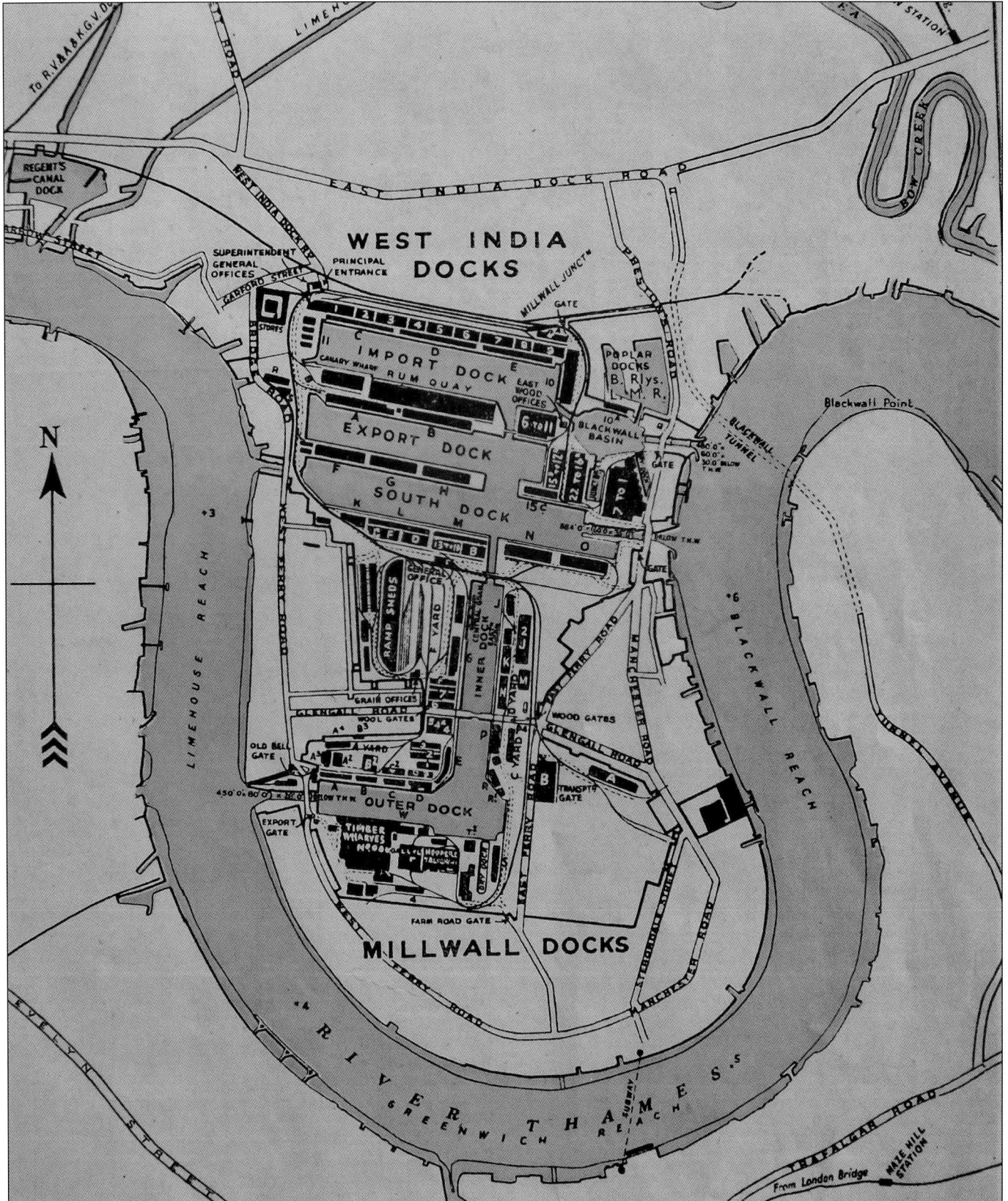

West India and Millwall Docks 1950s.

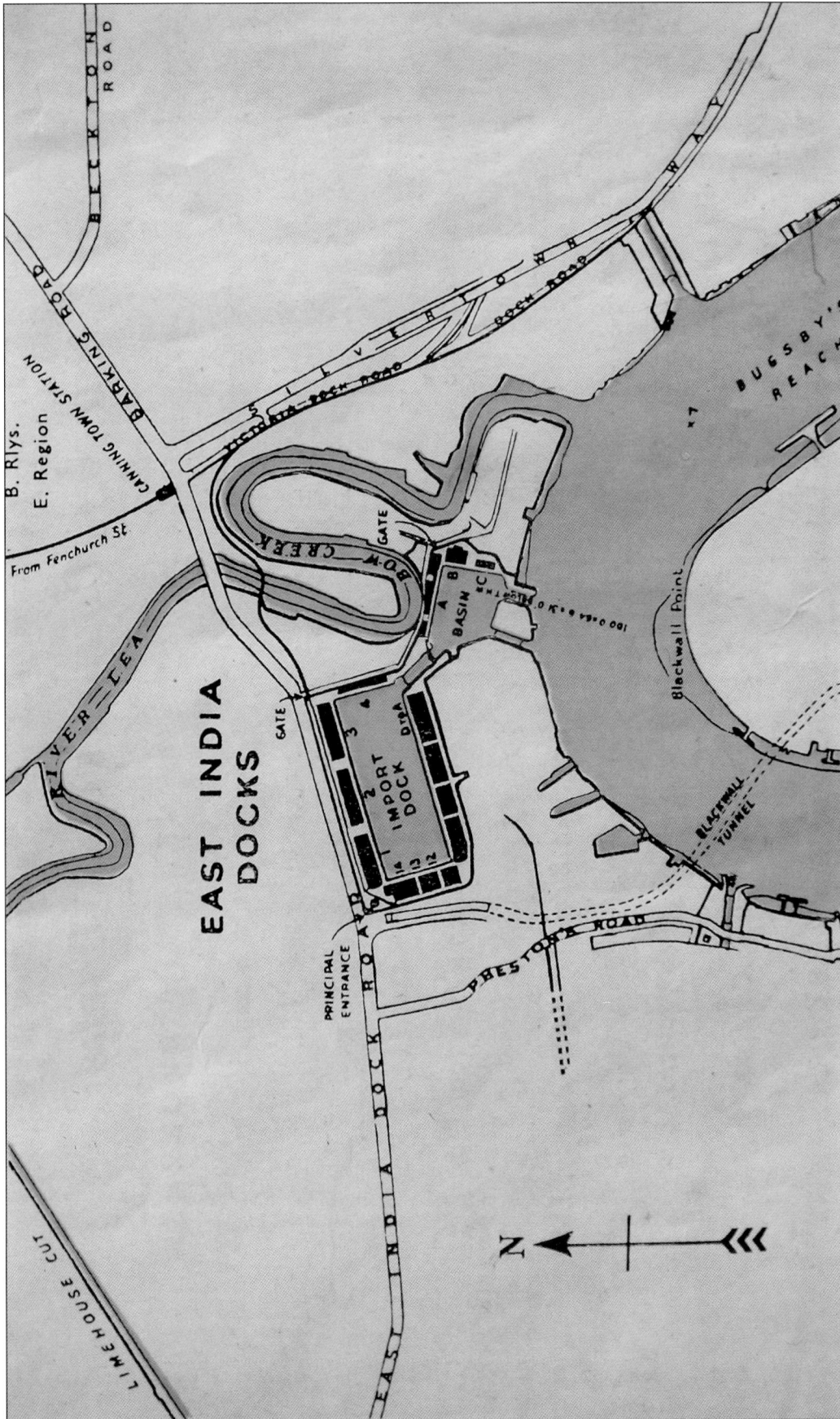

East India Dock and Limehouse Basin 1950s.

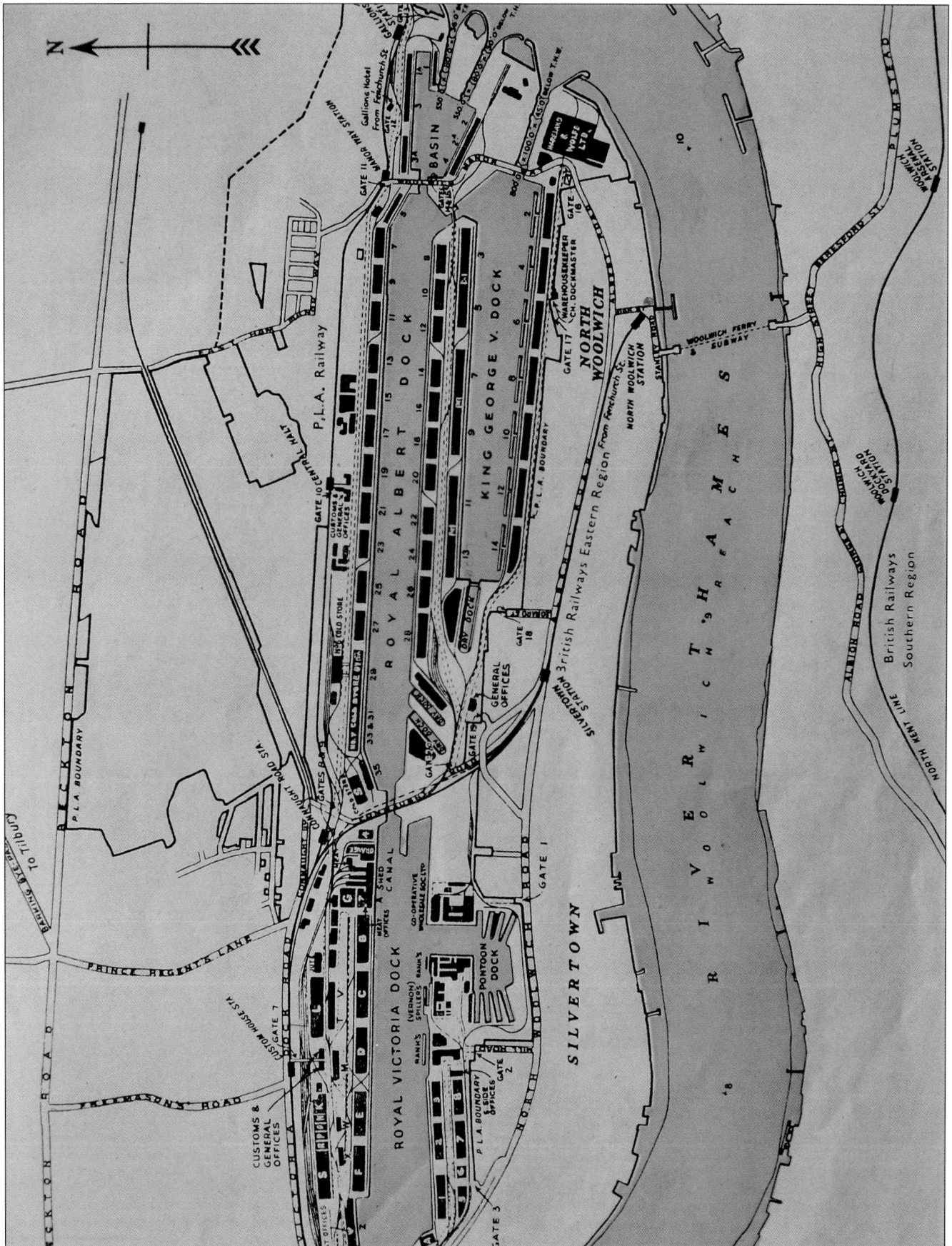

The Royal Docks 1950s.

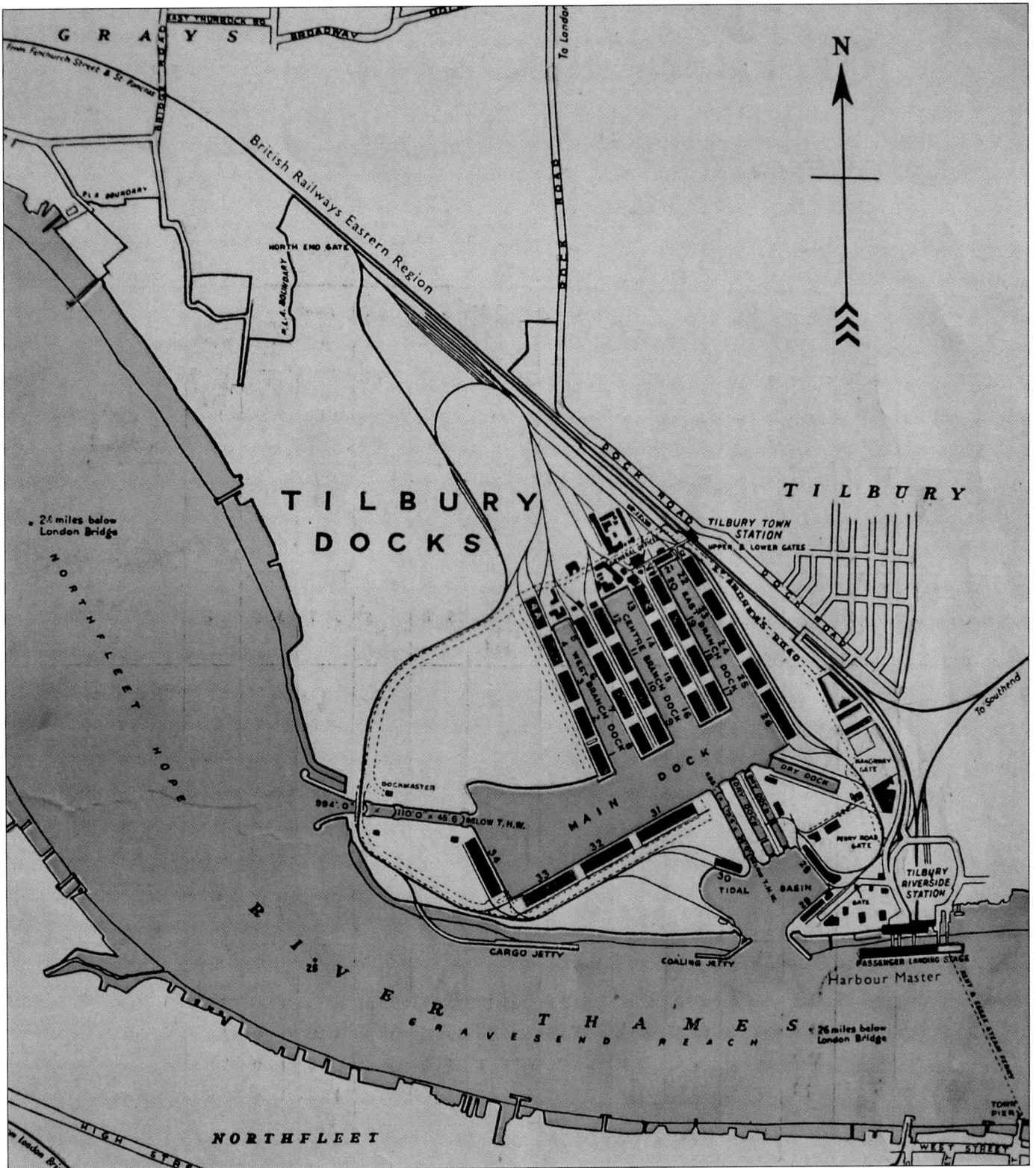

Tilbury Dock 1950s The Tidal Basin entrance was closed following 1960s expansion.

London's vanished dockside heritage – cranes and cargo handling methods

Most of the major changes to transport infrastructure and cargo handling have occurred in the last 50–60 years. The opening of the first section of the M1 motorway in 1959 signalled the start of a public commitment to road rather than rail internal transport. Commercial jet airliners, introduced in the 1950s, were to bring about an end of trans-ocean passenger shipping services (although in part replaced by cruising). International freight handling was to be revolutionised by the advent of containerisation from the 1960s.

Docks, like other parts of the transport infrastructure have had to adapt to these changes. Structures and working practices, which in 1960 might have seemed little changed from those of 1900, have been completely swept away since then. Until the middle of the nineteenth century there was little or no mechanised handling of cargoes. Goods tended to be carried on and off the small sailing ships or hoisted by means of a yardarm rig with a hand-operated winch. Some cranes would have had a fixed jib worked by a hand winch or treadmill. An example of a treadmill crane dating from the seventeenth century is preserved at Harwich. This would have been used for victualling naval craft.

The steamships which came increasingly into use after 1850 were more costly to build and operate than sail, so rapid turn-round times became more imperative. Steam derricks and winches began to be fitted to ships and some steam cranes on quaysides – but it was the use of hydraulic power rather than steam that was to make the greater impact on port development and cargo handling.

Hydraulic power was introduced into dockside use by William Armstrong in a demonstration installation on Newcastle's Town Quay in 1846. After successful further development, its use spread rapidly. The system worked by having a steam pumping station pump water into the vertical cylinder of an accumulator tower. A weighted ram was attached to the cylinder, and when water was pumped in this ram rose to the top of its stroke. Using water to power a crane or other application caused the ram to fall. Water could be supplied through a network of cast iron mains at a pressure of around 600–700psi. Remote accumulators on the network could be used to maintain the pressure. This was more efficient than having steam cranes, each of which had to have its own boiler and firebox.

Hydraulic power was introduced in London by the North London Railway at Poplar Docks in 1851–2 to work coal derricks. Regents Canal Dock followed, also using hydraulics for coal derricks in 1853. The sea-borne coal trade was under competition from rail-hauled coal brought by the newly opened Great Northern Railway. Other dock companies soon adopted the hydraulic system, so that by 1857 it was in use in all docks on the north side of the Thames, either on existing quays or as part of new developments, such as Victoria Dock in 1855. On the south side, the Surrey Commercial Dock didn't adopt hydraulic power until 1872.

Several of the small riverside wharves also introduced hydraulic power. As smaller hydraulic networks were less economic, there were soon moves to provide a common supply. The London Hydraulic Power Company set up its first pumping station in 1883. Eventually it was providing power for London, St Katharine, Surrey Commercial and East India Docks (taking over the existing pumping station there) and providing standby power for West India Docks and Millwall Docks.

Private wharf owners were encouraged to use LHP's supply by virtue of lower fire insurance rates than if they ran their own supply system. LHP also supplied a wide range of other users in London. The railway companies were also avid users of hydraulic power, with many dockland goods depots having their own pumping stations and accumulator towers.

The earliest hydraulically powered cranes were of the 'quay box' type. These were fixed cranes with a timber box housing to protect the hydraulic equipment and a jib mounted on the side on a corner pillar. On coal derricks the jib was pivoted to allow vertical movement (luffing), but most other cranes only had horizontal jib movement (slewing).

Portable cranes, moving on rails, were introduced in the 1870s. These afforded better access to ships' holds and were soon generally adopted, although luffing portables were not in wide-scale use in the docks until the 1900s.

By then quay cranes had evolved to be capable of four movements – hoisting, slewing, luffing and travelling. These travelling cranes were set on a portal straddling the roadway or railway line between the rails on which the crane travelled. The operator's position would be high up so as to see down into the ships' holds. At St Katharine Dock the warehouses were built right up to the quayside, leaving no space for quayside cranes, so wall cranes were attached to the warehouses and hydraulic jiggers were fitted to operate them. These were supplemented by portable jiggers known as 'hydraulic devils' which could be connected to hydrants to draw their power. Made by Armstrong's of Newcastle, these were introduced in the 1860s, falling out of use by the 1920s. An example of one of the cranes is preserved, attached to the wall of the Guoman Tower Hotel.

Some of the early cranes were supplied by the Armstrong company, which was also the chief supplier of the pumping engines and accumulating equipment. For instance, in 1867–8 it supplied Millwall Dock with one 15-ton capacity crane, two of 5 tons and twelve of 35cwt. Other suppliers included Tannet Walker & Co. of Leeds and the locally based East Ferry Road Engineering Works Co. Ltd. By 1900 there were sixty-five hydraulic cranes at Millwall Dock alone, while Poplar Dock had seventy-three. Most of the travelling cranes were of around 35cwt capacity.

Hydraulic power was versatile enough for other uses around the docks. Grain elevators, conveyers and tea bulking machines were so powered, providing some of the first examples of bulk handling of cargoes. Items of dock infrastructure such as capstans, lock gates and swing or lifting bridges were also hydraulically operated.

Further mechanisation became possible with the onset of electric power at the end of the century. Conveyer belt systems were in use for discharging tea crates and frozen meat by 1912. In 1920 Claud Scrutton designed a battery-powered platform truck which proved highly successful and was soon in general use.

Electric cranes and winches began to supplement, and then replace, hydraulic power on both the PLA quays and private wharves. Electric quay cranes were introduced to the Royal Docks in 1916, and for the opening of the King George V Dock on 8 July 1921 forty-two new electric cranes were supplied by Babcock & Wilcox Ltd. They had a reach of 26ft and a one-ton lifting capacity. These were mounted on seven reinforced concrete jetties or 'dolphins', each 520ft long and 32ft from the quay wall. Lighters could be moored between the jetty and the quayside, and ships could then discharge either on to the quayside or into lighters either at the jetty or the other side of the ship (using the ship's derricks). This feature was unique to this dock.

Some hydraulic cranes were converted to electric power, while others remained in use alongside their electric cousins into the 1960s. In 1962, when the docks were at peak capacity and before the containerisation revolution was to start the programme of closures, the PLA docks had between them a total of 438 electric cranes (of 2 to 5 ton capacity) and 117 hydraulic cranes (20–35cwt capacity). Five fixed heavy lift cranes and 208 mobile cranes were also in use, along with 115 fork-lift trucks and 230 electric trucks.

The mobile cranes included forty-five of the Jones KL77 model. In the Surrey Commercial Docks they were being used along with fork-lift trucks to stack timber in place of the traditional deal porters who had manually stacked the sawn timber, known as 'deals', in piles up to 12ft high, carrying the timbers precariously up narrow plankways. Fork-lift trucks and pallets began to be used from 1951 onwards, and although effective on quaysides and in warehouses were of limited use on board ships. However, new ships were fitted with larger hatches to accommodate pallets.

The latest type of electric quayside cranes being installed at this time was the DD2 type, manufactured by Stothart & Pitt of Bath, with Allen West control gear. These had an 80-foot radius suitable for wide-beamed cargo ships and had a far more streamlined appearance than their predecessors.

Five-ton electric cranes were used to unload hardwood logs and bulk sugar. Sugar had originally been transported in sacks, but by the 1960s it was shipped in bulk and unloaded by grab cranes. This still remains the case today at Tate & Lyle's refinery wharf at Silvertown.

The fixed heavy lift cranes were scattered around the dock network. Tilbury Dock had a dry dock 752ft long by 110ft wide equipped with a 40-ton crane, while West India Dock had a 10-ton example. The Royal Albert Dock had a berth with a 25-ton capacity travelling crane.

For the really big lifting jobs that were too heavy for the quayside cranes or ship's derricks to handle, the PLA also had a number of self-propelled heavy lift floating cranes, capable of working within the docks or on the river as required.

Conventional mobile cranes and excavators were (and still are) employed on maintenance and could be lifted on to floating pontoons to be towed to the work site. Private contractors' plant is also used. The PLA is also responsible for dredging the tidal Thames and used to have its own dredging craft, some having grab cranes as part of their equipment. Nowadays private dredging contractors are used.

Millwall and Royal Victoria Docks handled substantial traffic in bulk grain unloading to both privately-owned mills and a PLA-owned granary. As well as quayside elevators, in 1962 the PLA owned eight floating pneumatic grain elevators for unloading grain into lighters. Five of these had a discharge capacity of 200 tons per hour under the control of one operator. They were built by Spencer Handling Plant of Melksham, Wiltshire. However, grain-handling facilities were transferred to a new purpose-built terminal at Tilbury in 1969.

The main impediment to speeding loading and unloading times and reducing manpower was the need to make up and break down general cargo and organise its stowage within a ship's hold. If the ship was loading for more than one destination the cargo should ideally be stowed in port rotation order to avoid unnecessary handling movements when unloading, but there was also the need to stow cargo in such a way that the ship remained in trim and stable. There was also the need to keep incompatible commodities apart. All this created much work for the export packing companies who made crates and other packaging for products, and the gangs of dockers and crane drivers who loaded and unloaded the cargo under the supervision of the stevedores who organised the stowage. Industrial relations were poor in an industry long dominated by casual employment (as required) rather than a regular wage, and stoppages for disputes were frequent.

Another important consideration was that throughout the period a large proportion of cargo was unloaded into smaller craft and lighters for transfer to private wharves and warehouses rather than being unloaded to the dock quays.

Roll-on, Roll-off techniques started with the use of wartime tank-landing craft (LSTs). Tilbury was the first port in Britain to operate them when the Atlantic Steam Navigation Company started running between there and Rotterdam in 1946. The company's first purpose-built vessels came in 1959. There was a service from Tilbury–Antwerp from 1955. Services transferred from Tilbury to Felixstowe in 1968. They also had services between Preston and Ireland, and later became part of European Ferries. The concept developed rapidly in the 1960s with two special berths for such traffic being provided at Tilbury from 1966, with ramps for vehicles to drive on and off vessels through the bow and stern doors. This killed off much of the short-sea traffic from upstream London.

The main revolution was to come with containerisation from the late 1960s. Needing only a crane to lift and stack the containers, a ship could be loaded and unloaded in hours rather than days. After container sizes were standardised internationally in 1965, the PLA commissioned a report on Britain's export trade. It concluded in 1966 that a container port would be needed, or else shipping could be lost to European ports, as Antwerp and Rotterdam were also developing facilities.

Tilbury was chosen because the PLA had a lot of undeveloped land there, and there was good road and rail access, thus avoiding London congestion. Construction proceeded through 1967–8, and in January 1968 the initial service started to Rotterdam. In June the trans-Atlantic service was inaugurated by the new United States Lines' *American Lancer*. The berth for this was equipped with two 30-ton Paceco-Vickers cranes each costing £20,000, and a fleet of straddle carriers to stack the containers. Turnround time was within 24 hours, as opposed to 10–14 days for conventional cargo handling.

Meanwhile a consortium of shipping companies had formed Overseas Containers Ltd (OCL) and ordered nine new vessels for 1969 delivery for services between Europe and Australia. Tilbury was chosen as the European terminal. A new berth was ready for this by February 1969. However, this did not open until May 1970 when agreement was reached with the dockers. OCL's *Jervis Bay* worked the first service. By 1972 Tilbury had become the leading container-handling port in the UK and had achieved second place in Europe with a total of 231,438 containers handled, and with services to thirty overseas ports. In 1977 this had grown to 294,500 containers handled.

In 1978 the dock facilities were supplemented by a new riverside container-handling berth built on reclaimed land at Northfleet Hope. A railway Freightliner terminal had first opened at Tilbury in 1969 and this was also connected. There were Freightliner trains running from here as far as Glasgow and Liverpool.

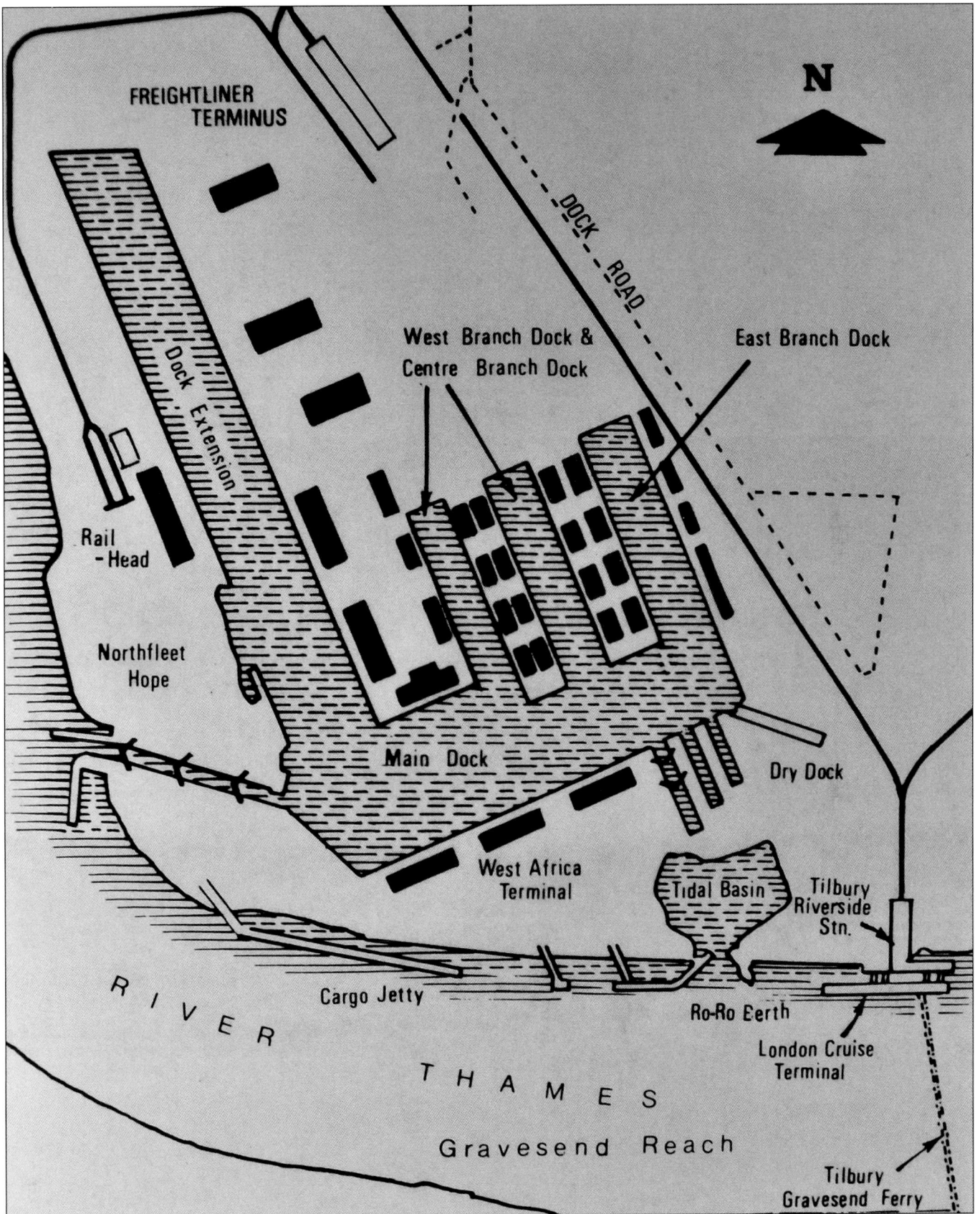

FREIGHTLINER TERMINUS

Dock Extension

West Branch Dock & Centre Branch Dock

East Branch Dock

DOCK ROAD

N

Rail-Head

Northfleet Hope

Main Dock

Dry Dock

West Africa Terminal

Tidal Basin

Tilbury Riverside Stn.

Cargo Jetty

Ro-Ro Berth

London Cruise Terminal

R I V E R   T H A M E S

Gravesend Reach

Tilbury Gravesend Ferry

Tilbury Docks 1980.

The main pumping station of the London Hydraulic Power Company at Wapping by the entrance to the former London Docks. This remained in use until 1977 and has since reopened as an arts centre and restaurant complex. Seen in 2013. *Photo by Malcolm Batten.*

Plaque on the wall of the London Hydraulic Power Company pumping station. *Photo by Malcolm Batten.*

A now disused hydraulically powered lifting bridge at the Shadwell Basin entrance to the former London Docks, closed in 1968. *Photo by Malcolm Batten.*

A preserved example of a hydraulic wall crane and jigger at St Katharine Dock – a design unique in London to this dock. *Photo by Malcolm Batten.*

GEOGRAPHICAL – DOCKS VIEWS

The Pool of London

The Upper Pool looking from Tower Bridge towards London Bridge in the distance, September 1949. In the foreground is Olsen & Ugelstad (Fjell Line) *Ornefjell*, built 1937 at 1,334 gross tons. This was sold off in 1955. Note the proliferation of lighters to take cargo off to the various riverside wharves and warehouses. The Upper Pool closed to commercial shipping c.1970.

Steam tug *Sunrise*, built 1928, 102 tons gross, belonging to W. H. J. Alexander Ltd (Sun Tugs), tows the Ellerman Wilson Line SS *Dago* (1947, 2,302grt) from its berth in the Upper Pool in September 1949.

Tower Bridge looking east with Butlers Wharf beyond. When built in 1894 this was the only bridge east of London Bridge and would remain so until the Queen Elizabeth II bridge opened at Dartford in October 1991.

On the same day, ships are seen on Butlers Wharf in the 1950s. Butlers Wharf closed in 1972. A consortium led by Terence Conran bought much of the site for conversion to flats and offices.

West India Docks

A view into West India Dock from the bridge at the entrance lock in Prestons Road. Ellerman Lines *City of York* (1976, 10,801grt) is in the foreground. Beyond this is one of P&O's 'Strath' class ships. 1977.

On the same day, the Port of London Authority's pusher tug *Broodbank* is entering the lock. In the distance can be seen one of the PLA's floating heavy lift cranes, the *London Mammoth*.

The 'Blue bridge' at the entrance to West India Docks. This was opened in 1969 and uses electric pumps and oil hydraulics. It is the sixth successive bridge to have been built on this site. A London Transport DMS Fleetline crosses the bridge on 8 October 1978. The dock closed in 1980 but remains open for shipping, often foreign warships on courtesy visits. *Photo by Malcolm Batten.*

Royal Docks

Swedish Lloyd *Britannia* (1929, 4,216grt) in King George V Dock c.1949. The cranes seen are probably the originals. With her sister *Suecia* they operated a cargo/passenger service to Gothenburg, passengers boarding at Tilbury. Both ships were sold in 1966 to Hellenic Mediterranean Lines.

A busy scene in King George V Dock in the early 1950s. At this time many of the ships would also convey some passengers, but this traffic would largely be lost to air travel by the end of the 1960s.

Another 1950s general view of King George V Dock. The cranes have now been replaced by more modern examples.

Another busy scene from the 1950s, with the Suisse-Atlantique Line *General Guisan* (1957, 9,054grt) nearest in view.

Into the 1960s now, and many of the dockside cranes have been replaced by newer DD2 models made by Stothart & Pitt of Bath. A pair of Blue Star Line ships dominate, with *Ulster Star* (1959, 9,695grt) being the closest.

A scene from the early 1980s. Possibly a Sunday as none of the cranes are working. The black-hulled ship is the *Belloc*. This was owned by Lamport & Holt (1980, 9,324grt).

Entry into the Royal Docks was through the lock entrance from Gallions Reach into KGV Dock. Alexandra Towing Co. tug *Sun XXIV* (1962, 120grt) seen in 1976 with Nedlloyd's *Loire Lloyd* (1967, 9,638grt).

China Shipping *Dongming* (1964, 10,421grt) waits in the lock for the water levels to adjust, 1978. This was ex the *Sea Amber* in 1973.

The bascule bridge on Woolwich Manor Way has opened and a pair of PLA tugs with *Plankton* (1965, 122grt) on the right pass through from the lock into the dock.

The bascule bridge on Woolwich Manor Way. The bridge was built by Sir William Arrol & Co. Ltd of Glasgow. Buses on route 101 Wanstead–North Woolwich would often be held here as the bridge was lifted for ships to enter and leave the docks, giving upstairs passengers a grandstand view but a long wait. As a result, the route was operated in two overlapping sections, Wanstead to Royal Albert Dock, and Manor Park to North Woolwich to even out the frequency on the northern section of the route.

By contrast, a swing bridge gave access for shipping between King George V Dock and the Royal Albert Dock. Both these bridges were worked by hydraulic power. Two of the PLA's heavy lift floating cranes can be seen in this view.

Having passed through the lock, and with PLA tug *Plankton* on her stern, New Zealand Line's *NZ Aorangi* (1967, 12,227grt) is swung round to pass through the swing bridge into the Royal Albert Dock and beyond that, the Royal Victoria Dock, in 1975. This was formerly Shaw Savill Line *Majestic* until 1974.

What comes in must go out… Sun tug *Sun XXIV* brings *Pointe des Colibris* (1969, 6,738grt) into the lock in 1976. This was owned by French Line C.G.T.

Riverside wharves and moorings

The Regents Canal Dock, operated by the British Waterways Board at Limehouse Basin, was where goods could be transhipped from sea-going craft to canal barges for transport via the Regents Canal around London and on to the Midlands. The dock was closed in 1967 and was later redeveloped for housing and as a marina. In 1979 the *Artemis K* (1944, 2,883grt), a Panamanian registered former ferry was berthed along with paddle tug *Hero* and tugs *Goliath* and *Cervia*. *Artemis K* had been owned by Marine Transport Lines (USA) as the *Artemis*, previously *Myconos,* and had been converted from a seaplane tender. The tugs were stored for preservation. *Hero* was built in 1931 for the Tees Conservancy and was the last paddle tug to be built in the UK for a civilian owner. She later passed to the Medway Maritime Museum under her original name of *John H. Amos. Cervia* passed to the East Kent Maritime Museum at Ramsgate.

Henry Tate opened a refinery at Silvertown in 1878 to refine cane sugar. Later merging with Abram Lyle to form Tate & Lyle, both this and Abram Lyle's refinery (also in Silvertown) remain in use and still receive some forty ships a year. Bulk carriers are unloaded by grab cranes discharging into hoppers, replacing the former carriage in sacks. In 1982 *Jagat Priya* (1975, 13,390grt) owned by Dempo Steamships, India was being unloaded.

On another later occasion the Japanese owned Tokumaru K. K. (Tokai Line) *Fresh Ocean* (1974, 3,572grt) was on the wharf.

Coaster *Isabel Mitchell* (1956, 298grt) at Cawoods Mast Pond Wharf, Woolwich,1981. At the time owned by H. R. Mitchell, she was on her fifth name, having started as the *Helge* until 1964.

Firethorn (1967, 1,041grt) at Deptford Creek in 1981. The '– thorn' coasters of William Coe had amalgamated with the '– M' coasters of Metcalf Motor Coasters in 1978 to form Coe Metcalf Shipping. The building in the background is Deptford West power station, built in 1929 and closed in 1983.

Coaster *Aat-V* (1962, 499grt) at Mast Pond Wharf. Owned by International Shipbrokers she had been the *Breezand* until 1973.

William Cory Bros leased a wharf just beyond Gallions station at North Woolwich. Passenger services on this line ceased in September 1940 following air-raid damage, but the wharf was still accessible by PLA tracks through the Royal Docks. The cranes would be used to unload coal brought by ship from the northeast for onward road or rail distribution to London and the southeast, including probably Rye House Power Station, Broxbourne. Note the Sentinel shunter.

Various ships moored at Woolwich in 1975. Bowker & King Ltd coastal tankers *Blackpool* (1962, 530grt) in foreground with *Bacarrat* (1959, 293grt) behind. A spare Woolwich ferry is moored mid-river. A ship is on the Tate & Lyle's refinery wharf. The Thames Flood Barrier now crosses the river just beyond Tate & Lyle.

Lighters in Bow Creek, 1950s.

Lighters at wharves on the River Lea at Bow, 1950s.

J. Brunvall, Norway *Brunhorn* (1973, 5,643grt) unloading rolls of newsprint paper at Imperial Wharf, Gravesend, owned by the Imperial Paper Mills at the time. 1982.

Tilbury

A general view looking across the river from Gravesend. An outward-bound tanker passes China Shipping's cargo ship *Qianjin* (1965, 6,888grt) on the cargo jetty. In the background can be seen the container cranes of Northfleet Hope container terminal, just round the bend. On the right the funnel of a vessel in the dock is visible. 1981.

Northfleet Hope container terminal opened in 1978. Australian National Line's *Australian Venture* (1977, 43,878grt) was a caller here in 1980.

Unloading grain in 1980 from the bulk carrier *Amber Pacific* (1969, 31,409grt) at the Tilbury Grain terminal, which opened in 1969. She was owned by Seahorse Ship Management.

Vasa Shipping of Finland are the owners of *Sandviken* (1962, 9,329grt) which unloads at the cargo jetty in 1980. This was built in 1929 for ships just discharging part of their cargo to avoid entering the dock. Stothert & Pitt cranes are on the jetty.

Gorthon Lines (Sweden) *Tilia Gorthon* (1975, 7,283grt) is stern to stern with *Sandviken*. When built this jetty was 1,000ft long.

Tilbury Passenger Landing stage was opened in May 1930 measuring 1,142 feet long. Seen in 1979.

Tilbury Landing Stage hosts Russian cruise ship *Antonina Nezhdanov* in 1982.

The ramp leading to Tilbury landing stage.

The Ocean Liner Terminal building in 1982. By the 1980s, passengers for cruises were being brought by coach rather than by special boat trains from St Pancras. The Landing Stage was refurbished in 1989 and renamed the London International Cruise Terminal.

Tilbury Riverside station clock tower. Note the weathervane (since removed) in the shape of an LMS 'Royal Scot' locomotive. The company worked boat trains from St Pancras to Tilbury although the motive power was likely to be more mundane! In February 1990 British Rail put forward proposals to close the station and in early 1992 a public enquiry took place to assess the proposal. BR claimed a saving of £1.5m could be made in infrastructure renewal as against revenue of £11,000 a year. The Secretary of State granted approval on condition a connecting bus to Tilbury Town was provided, and so the station was closed on 29 November 1992.

The collier sighting station at Tilbury. In the days before telephones, messengers would be sent from here on horseback to London with the latest news on ship arrivals. 1977.

Tilbury waterfront didn't only attract ship photographers! 1976.

Infrastructure work

The Thames Flood Barrier under construction. Completed in 1982 at a cost of £535m it was officially opened by HM the Queen on 8 May 1984.

An excavator reinforces sea wall defences at Tilbury in 1979.

CARGO SHIPPING

Thames barges

Sailing on – Thames sailing barges

The origins of the sailing barges were dictated by the geography of the area they served, in particular that of Essex. On the river Thames, from the Middle Ages onwards, sea-going ships would moor in mid-stream to avoid grounding on the mud alongside the wharves at low tide, and because of insufficient wharfage space. Lighters would tranship the goods to the wharves, and also upriver where the ships could not go, above London Bridge and up the shallow tributary rivers such as the Lea and Medway as far as Maidstone. Even when enclosed docks were constructed in the nineteenth century this practice continued, partly because the lighters provided a form of cheap warehousing. Other Essex rivers giving access to the North Sea such as the Colne, Crouch and Blackwater were also navigable only to a craft of shallow draught, so again goods were transhipped into lighters near the river mouth for onward passage.

These broad, box-shaped lighters had a high cargo capacity, and being flat-bottomed would stay upright when grounded at low water. The crew, never more than two, would propel them using large poles and making use of the tidal flow. Some owners later added a squaresail to run before the wind on longer journeys, thus evolving into a different type of vessel – the barge. The masts could be lowered to pass under bridges. However, barges like this could not go to windward, i.e. sail against the wind, so without a following wind would be dependent on the tides. To overcome this limitation various types of sail arrangement were tried such as the lug sail and the gaff & boom. Eventually the spritsail rig was found to be the most practical and economic and the distinctive form of the sailing barge had arrived.

Up to the beginning of the nineteenth century barges were probably unable to go to sea. The greatest developments, taking them into the form we know today, occurred between 1800 and the 1920s. Indeed, the golden age of barging could be said to have started when, in 1863, Henry Dodd initiated an annual barge sailing match. This was an immediate success, and within ten years barges were being designed with racing specifically in mind.

As finally developed the typical barge was around 80–90ft long, about 21ft wide, and with a draught of around 3ft 6in. The average payload ranged from 80–200 tons, though some of the largest built carried nearer 300 tons. The characteristic spritsail rig featured a large spar or sprit attached near the foot of the mast and extending diagonally back. On a large barge this might be some 65ft in length, of timber, or latterly steel tube. The sprit crossed the mainsail diagonally, supporting the sail at its upper outer end.

The number and type of sails varied on different barges. Some carried a mainsail, foresail and mizzen, the so-called 'stumpy rig'. Some had a boom & gaff type sail on the mizzen – these were referred to as 'mulie rigged'. Spritsail barges had mainsail, foresail, topsail, staysail and mizzen. The largest 'boomie' barges were a cross between a schooner and a barge – ketch rigged with a bowsprit and jibs and sometimes mizzen topsails. They were referred to as 'schooners with the bottom cut off' and were designed for the coastal coal trade. The sails of barges were dressed with a mixture of oil and ochre giving them their distinctive reddish-brown colour.

On all barges, the masts of course, continued to be capable of lowering to enable the barge to pass under bridges. Some crews could sail up to a bridge, lower the gear, 'shoot' through, and heave up again without stopping. The hulls were built of oak and/or pitch pine, and in later years, iron or steel. Wheel steering began to replace the tiller from the 1870s.

As the barges were flat bottomed and of shallow draught they would be liable to make leeway (go sideways) when working to windward. To prevent this, sailing craft normally have a keel to get a grip on the water, but fitting one of these would have defeated the barge's accessibility advantage. So instead they were fitted with a large 'leeboard' hung on each side of the hull, which could be raised or lowered depending on which tack the barge was sailing. They were lowered on the leeward side. The leeboards were fan-shaped, from 10–17ft long and 6–7ft wide at their widest point. in early days they were controlled by a tackle, in later years by winches.

All these developments of the original dumb lighter contrived to produce a craft that was quite capable of withstanding rough sea conditions: able to sail across the Channel or even the North Sea, and then capable of taking its cargo upriver where no sailing hoy or smack or steamboat could venture. There was no fuel cost and crewing costs were minimal. The barges were normally worked with just two or three crew – a skipper, mate and boy – or four on the largest 'boomie' barges. The large hatches enabled quick turnrounds. Often the crew unloaded and loaded their craft in a single day. It was dusty and backbreaking labour for the crews, bringing extra pay to supplement their low wages. No tugs were needed in dock, and when empty, the barges' broad flat-bottomed layout gave them the stability to sail without taking on ballast. Once under way the barges were fast, even in light winds. They could make twelve knots when racing. Thus, the sailing barges had an economic advantage that kept them in business long after sail had been displaced elsewhere.

The rapid expansion of London's urban population led to growth in trade and a demand for foodstuffs. The Thames barges carried a wide variety of cargoes. Straw, grain, timber, bricks and cement were all typical loads. Wheat imported from Canada and Europe was transhipped from London to millers on the rivers Stour and Orwell amongst others. Hay was brought from the farms of Essex and Suffolk to feed and bed the thousands of horses working in London before motorised transport.

Other barges were engaged in the coastal coal trade, especially the 'boomies'. But they were later displaced by the more economical 'mulies', needing only three as opposed to four crew members. Indeed the four largest spritsail barges built were all designed for this traffic, delivering to Margate gasworks, although they carried other goods as well. These were built in 1925–6 for the well-known firm of F. T. Everard & Sons of Greenhithe. The quartet, named *Alf Everard*, *Ethel Everard*, *Fred Everard* and *Will Everard*, were 97ft 6in long, 23ft wide and had a payload of around 280 tons. They were steel hulled and mulie rigged. *Ethel Everard* was abandoned at Dunkirk during the evacuation, *Alf* and *Fred* both sank in the 1950s by which time they had been converted to motor power, but *Will Everard* (now just *Will*) lives on.

By contrast some small barges known as 'cut barges' were built to fit the locks on London's Regent canal, bringing building materials to wharves in north London.

Barges were operated by a number of companies, large and small, and by owner-skippers. One of the largest of the general companies, The London & Rochester Trading Co. (originally the Rochester Barge Co.), was formed by the barge builders Gill Brothers. They had a new barge on their hands when a client went bankrupt, started trading with her, and found this more profitable than barge building. By 1900 they had twenty-five barges and the fleet continued to expand by takeovers into the 1950s. They later became a major operator of motor coasters and changed their name to Crescent Trading. Other major companies include F. T. Everard & Sons of Greenhithe, who, as previously mentioned had the largest barges built active in the coal trade. E. J. & W. Goldsmith of Grays regularly carried timber from Surrey Commercial Docks to Ipswich. Francis & Gilders of Colchester had fifteen barges under sail in 1949 but merged with London & Rochester Trading in 1951.

The heyday of barging was at around the turn of the century when there were some 2,000 barges registered. But some traffic was already being lost to the railways, such as coal from Newcastle. The depression years of the 1920s and '30s hit the barging trade hard with many craft being laid up, for instance at 'Starvation Point' off North Woolwich. Competition was also being faced increasingly from purpose-built motor coasters, many overseas owned, which were penetrating the coastal trade. These were easier to load and unload with their absence of rigging. Some of the barge owners started to fit auxiliary engines to their craft from around 1930 onwards. The expansion of road transport also hit the coasting trade as goods could be transported direct to their consignee. The brick trade lost out to lorries that delivered direct to the builder's yard or building site.

After the Second World War some 200 sailing barges survived. Many were in need of extensive repairs. Timber suitable for masts and sprits was virtually unobtainable and sails had more than trebled in price. Crewing became more difficult as fewer young men were willing to take on the work.

Many of the smaller fleet owners and owner-skippers dropped out, although some of the biggest fleets like London & Rochester Trading continued to expand through takeovers. There was still regular traffic in grain to Ipswich and Whitstable, sand and ballast to London etc. More of the barges were fitted with engines, losing much or even all of their rigging in the process to become fully powered craft.

Barges continued to be rapidly withdrawn or converted during the 1950s so much so that in 1956 there were only twenty-four barges trading actively under sail with around 100 fully converted to motor power. By 1961 the *Cambria* was the only unpowered barge in regular use. Sold by Everards to Bob Roberts as owner-skipper, he continued to work her until 1970 when, as the last barge to work under sail, she passed into the ownership of the newly formed Maritime Trust.

Above: A line-up of Thames barges await their next call to duty at Woolwich in the 1930s or 1940s.

Opposite above: A fine study of Thames barges laid up at 'Starvation Point', North Woolwich in the late 1930s or 1940s.

Opposite below: Looking the other way on the same day, and there are more Thames barges and an unidentified ship in mid-river.

A Thames barge unloading cargo into lighters at the entrance to the Royal Docks, Gallions Reach, Woolwich in 1948.

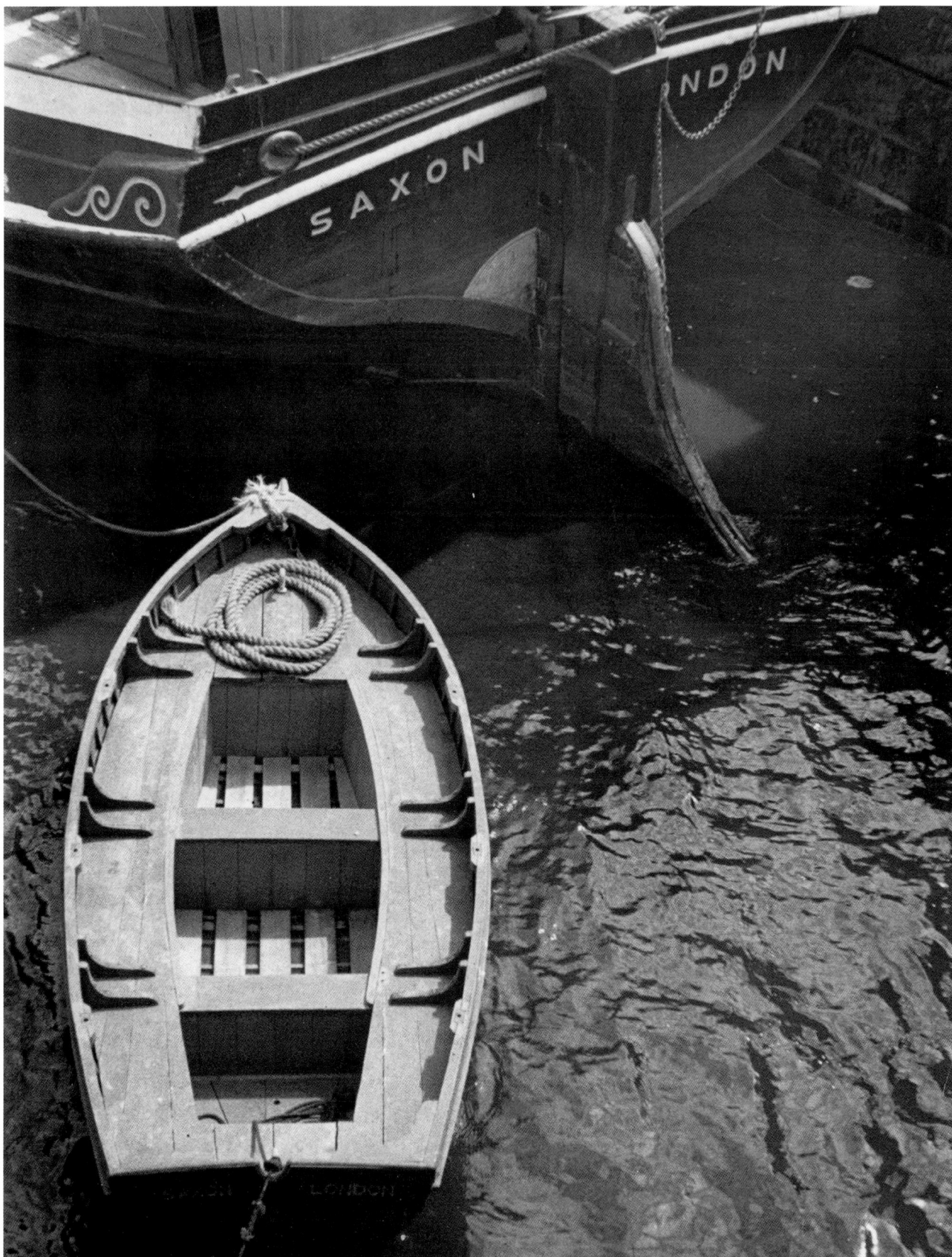

The stern of barge *Saxon*, with its accompanying dinghy taken near the power station at Woolwich in 1946.

The flat-bottomed design of the Thames barges enabled them to get right up the creeks and rivers of the Essex coast. Here a barge is seen at Marriage's Mill on the River Colne at the Hythe, Colchester, Essex.

General cargo vessels with derricks

Children play by the water's edge as a veteran of 1945, Hellenic Lines' *Cypros* (3,799grt) arrives at Tilbury on the incoming tide in 1976.

Passing Woolwich in 1976 is the *Balchik* (1949, 1,809grt) owned by Navigation Maritime Bulgare of Bulgaria. She was previously named *Nikola Vaptzarov*.

Hellenic Lines of Greece also owned the *Roumania* (1954, 3,654grt). This had been the *Prinses Maria* until 1970, and prior to that the *Van Waerwyck*. Tilbury, 1979.

Ben Line *Benledi* (1954, 8,800grt) in the KGV dock lock with PLA tug *Plangent* in attendance. The Harland & Wolff ship repair works can be seen alongside.

Samudera, Indonesia owned *Pratita* (1954, 6,900grt), ex Hapag-Lloyd *Isarstein* in 1973. Heading out from the 'Royals' in 1977.

Blue Star Line *Buenos Aires Star* (1956, 8,257grt) in 1977. Having departed the Royal Docks she is now heading downriver in Gallions Reach.

Fednav (Canada) *Tundraland* (1958, 3,349grt), seen in 1976.

Houlder Bros & Co Ltd. *Westbury* (1960, 8,414grt) is manoeuvred within King George V dock in 1977.

A year newer is Black Star Line, Ghana *Otchi River* (1961, 7,378grt). Tilbury, 1980.

Glen Line *Flintshire* (1962, 11,537grt). Gallions Reach, 1977.

P&O Line *Strathnaver* (1962, 9,890grt) ex *Jumna* (James Nourse) about to enter KGV lock.

Also from P&O and dating from 1962 is *Strathtay* (10,028grt) ex *Trebartha* (Hain SS Co.), 1977.

Clan Line *Clan MacGregor* (Glasgow) (1962, 8,811grt) is manoeuvred within KGV by PLA tug *Plasma*, 1978.

Sudan Line *Sennar* (1962, 3,741grt). Gallions Reach, 1979.

Escorted by a pair of Sun tugs, *Diaken Love* (1964, 6,169grt) approaches the entrance to the 'Royal' group of docks in 1977. She was with Diaken Shipping of Greece, formerly named *Concordia Love* and originally *Fernland* of Fearnley & Eger.

This is *Vaygach* (1965, 4507grt), one of many Russian owned ships that brought timber to London. These would have gone into the Surrey Docks until their closure in 1970.

Pakistani owned *Bagh-E-Dacca* (1966, 8,967grt) in 1976.

'Hansa' (Deutsche Dampfschiffahrts) *Hohenfels* (1967, 9,433grt) has containers as deck cargo within KGV, 1979.

Arya National Shipping Lines SA of Iran were the owners of *Arya Sara* (1967, 10,172grt). She was previously *Lucie Delmas*.

Harrison Line *Historian* (1968, 8,454grt). These Harrison Line ships could be recognised by their distinctive T shaped Velle mast at the stern. PLA tug *Plankton* is on the stern in 1977.

Sugar Line Ltd *Sugar Producer* (1968, 13,894grt). Sugar Line was formed by Tate & Lyle and the United Molasses Company in 1950 in response to the beginning of bulk transportation of cane sugar, which had previously been transported in sacks. Gallions Reach, 1977.

Hamburg Sudamerika *Polar Columbia* (1968, 5,623grt) – a very stylish looking ship with twin funnels. Passing Woolwich in 1976 she was on charter to Salenrederierna of Sweden and carrying their funnel markings.

At Tilbury in 1981 is *General A. F. Cebesoy* (1969, 10,058grt). Owners were D. B. Deniz Nakliyati of Turkey.

Awaiting entry to the KGV lock in 1977 is China Shipping *Anting* (1970, 9,796grt) ex the *Kunlunshan*. China Shipping would be one of the last companies to dock in the 'Royals'.

Passing Tilbury in 1982 is *Golden Venture* (1971, 10,067grt). She was owned by P. S. Li, Hong Kong.

China Shipping *Yulin* (1972, 9,758grt) in the KGV lock, 1979. On this occasion the PLA tug on the stern is the *Lord Devonport*, allocated to the dredging fleet, rather than one of the regular dock tugs.

Heading the other way is the Malaysian International Shipping Corporation's *Bunga Teratai* (1972, 11,460grt) in 1977.

Heading downriver passing Gravesend in 1981 is *Arpoador* (1973, 10,182grt). This was owned by Empresa de Nav. Alianca, Brasil.

Deutsche Seereederei (East Germany) *Suhl* (1976, 10,047grt) ex *Phenix 1* in 1979. Tilbury, 1982.

On charter to the Nigerian National Shipping Line in 1979 was the *Sol Tulla* (1977, 9,309grt) owned by Johannes Solstad, Norway. Outward bound and about to pass Tilbury Power Station she is laden with containers.

General cargo vessels with cranes

For a period some ships were built with a mixture of cranes and derricks such as Russian owned *Anatoly Lunacharskiy* (1971, 9,323grt) seen at Gravesend in 1981.

Bank Line *Meadowbank* (1973, 11,405grt) with cranes & derricks in 1977.

Ellerman Line *City of Winchester* (1976, 10,801grt) in 1978.

Pacific Steam Navigation (Furness Withy) *Orcoma* (1966, 10,300grt) in 1977. She was sold to Indonesia in 1979. Note containers as deck cargo.

Empresa de Nav. Alianca, Brasil *Olinda* (1972, 10,417grt) heads away from the Royal Docks, 1977.

Navale et Comm., Hauraise, France *Ville de Rouen* (1977, 16,505grt). Seen in 1982.

Also from Empresa de Nav. Alianca, Brasil *Ana Louisa* (1981, 8,680grt) an SD14 type passing Gravesend in 1982.

French Line C.G.T. *Pointe des Colibris* (1969, 6,738grt) in 1976. We saw this earlier in the KGV lock. (see p. 34)

Iraqi Line *Basrah* (1971, 9,859grt) seen under a stormy sky in 1977.

Cie. Nationale Algerienne of Algeria were the owners of *Biban* (1977, 11,665grt), entering the KGV lock in 1978 with containers.

On charter to Saguenay Shipping is the Greek owned *Sunmaria* (1978, 10,994grt) ex *Maria Angelicoussi* 1982. This was also carrying containers. Saguenay operated services from the UK to Canada and also to Trinidad and Barbados.

United Lines (Lundqvist) of Finland *Doris* (1967, 2,928grt). This would be one of the last such vessels to come to the Thames for these Scandinavian companies – the next generation of ships would be Ro-Ros. (see p. 125)

Denholm Ship Management (Canpark Shipping Co Ltd.) *Arctic Troll* (1971, 22,160grt) at Tilbury, 1979.

Bulk carriers

Norden's *Nordkap* (1975, 19,589grt) at Tilbury in 1982.

Alfred C. Toepfer, Germany *Warschau* (1976, 30,348grt) with a deck cargo of timber in 1981.

Polish Steamship Company *Miroslawiec* (1975, 20,593grt), 1982.

Fednav Ltd, Canada *Federal Schelde* (1977, 21,484grt) at Tilbury in 1979 possibly bound for the grain terminal.

Schlussel Rederi, Germany *Bischofstor* (1976, 21,685grt) anchored mid-river at Gravesend.

SCA, Sweden *Tunadal* (1967, 9,355grt) fitted with straddle gantry cranes, 1978.

Y. C. Cheng/The Star Shipping Group consortium owned *Star Enterprise* (1978, 25,077grt) taken in 1982.

P. S. Li, Hong Kong *Grand Reliance* (1968, 19,286grt) was ex Canadian Pacific *H. R. MacMillan* in 1978. Seen in 1980.

Anangel Shipping Enterprises of Greece were the owners of *Anangel Might* (1978, 13,889grt), on charter to Norasia Line in 1981.

Coasters and motor barges

Coastal shipping delivering cargoes to small river quays was once a mainstay of the British economy, challenged seriously only by the railways. Since 1945 the trade has been under attack on several fronts. The rise of road transport, offering door-to-door carriage with no transhipment, hit the smaller companies, often family-owned that traded to the up-river ports.

The British coastal trade was affected by the decline in coal use by power stations, industry, the railways and for home heating during the 1950s and '60s. British shipping was also hit by free trade rules allowing ships of all flags to compete, even for trade between UK ports.

The Dutch came to dominate the European coastal fleet in the first decade after the Second World War.

They were early to convert to diesel power, both new-built and former sailing craft. Initially most were family owned, working through an agency to secure cargoes and charters. They made full use of working to the limits of the regulations on tonnage which determined levels of dues and manning.

Technological improvements allowing a reduction in crew numbers included folding steel hatch covers replacing boards and tarpaulins, self-slewing derricks, automated engine room controls, and controllable-pitch propellers. Superstructure was concentrated aft to allow as much cargo space as possible. Larger coasters now served fewer ports with faster turnarounds, relying on onwards road distribution. The cost of these led to a near disappearance of the small family owning tradition in favour of larger companies.

Motor barge *Queenford* (1959, 200grt) owned by Thomas J. Palmer, 1979.

Motor barge *Andescol* (1961, 191grt) was part of the London & Rochester Trading/Crescent Shipping fleet.

Usborne & Sons *St Andrews* (1961, 437grt) ex *Johanne*. Tilbury, 1981.

Union Transport *Union Mars* (1981, 986grt) seen when new in 1981.

London & Rochester Trading Co. Ltd *Eminence* (1969, 999grt) off Delta Wharf, Greenwich, 1977.

London & Rochester Trading Co. Ltd *Sentence* (1974, 992grt), Tilbury, 1980.

R. Lapthorn & Co. Ltd. *Hoomoss* (1969, 400grt) ex *Kosmos* in 1979. They started business in 1951 with *Nellie*, a 1901 built, 110 tonne Thames sailing barge converted to a motor barge. This was used to ship aggregate from Grays in Essex to Hoo in Kent and was sold in 1960. In 2001 the company was operating twenty-four vessels, all British flagged, making it numerically the largest British-registered dry cargo fleet.

Mardolf Peach & Co. *Sarah Weston* (1975, 926grt) in Gallions Reach, 1977.

Mardolf Peach & Co. *Caroline Weston* (1974, 1,582grt) ex *Frendo Grace* leaves the Royal Docks, 1977.

Klondyke Shipping Co Ltd, Hull *Westondyke* (1971, 696grt), 1977.

Klondyke Shipping Co. Ltd, Hull *Somersbydyke* (1967, 1,600grt). Woolwich, 1977.

F. T. Everard & Sons Ltd *Rosemary Everard* (1965, 1,598grt) is moored alongside the *Lancasterbrook* of Comben Longstaff & Co Ltd, 1981.

Hibbert Shipping Co had the *Thamwell* (1963, 427grt), seen in 1982. Until 1981 this had been part of the Becks fleet as the *Victress*.

On charter to Prince Line as *Nordic Prince* was Hall Bros *Bretwalda* (1971, 1,587grt), 1977.

Northumbria Shipping's *Northumbria Lass* (1968, 498grt), Tilbury, 1982.

Eggar Forrester *Lu* (1980, 497grt) Tilbury, 1981.

The Irish fleet of Arklow Shipping are still regular visitors to the Thames in 2020. This was their *Arklow Castle* (1981, 1,054grt) in 1982.

Edgar Dorman (1978, 664grt) taken in Gallions Reach in 1980 was with Shamrock Shipping Co. Ltd, Larne, Ireland.

Bork Line, Germany *Wotan* (1978, 999grt), in 1981.

Georg Peterson, Germany were the owners of *Frauke Catharina* (1972, 499grt) passing Tilbury with a deck cargo of timber in 1979.

Also from Germany came the *Neunfelde* (1955, 424 grt) of W. B. Bartels, 1977.

Halstenbek (1960, 499grt) owned by Carsten Rehder, Germany, in 1977.

Becks Scheepvaartkantoor N. V., Holland *Electron* (1966, 383grt) passes Gravesend, 1978.

Becks Scheepvaartkantoor N.V., Holland *Noblesse* (1980, 1,000grt) is heading back to sea at Tilbury in 1981.

The *Fenix* (1977, 1,599grt) was owned by Lennart, Kihlberg, Sweden. Taken in 1979.

With a deck cargo of liquid canisters the *Magali* (1956, 654 grt) hailed from Spain. 1977.

Mascareigne Shipping & Trading, Mauritius *Rodriguez* (1965, 495grt) had just been acquired and renamed having previously been the *Dania*. She was on Imperial Wharf, Gravesend when photographed in 1981.

Colliers

When coal powered London

In the twenty-first century, the headlines are full of climate change stories. The effects on the world's climate of global warming caused by among other things the burning of fossil fuels is being seen as a threat that needs immediate attention. The scale and cost of changes needed to reduce this consumption is enormous. Already we have seen some substantial attempts to alleviate the situation by the establishment of wind farms as a source of 'green' renewable energy, but this is only the tip of the iceberg. The Climate Change Act 2008 committed the UK to an 80 per cent reduction in six greenhouse gases from a 1990 baseline by 2050.

Around fifty years ago, the situation was totally different. One fossil fuel, namely coal, dominated our requirements, as it had for the past 300 years or so. It provided direct heating for many of our homes, power for many of our factories, and fuel for most of our railway locomotives. It was also the principal source of fuel for the gasworks and power stations that provided us with our gas and electricity. However, it was in 1956 that Britain passed the first Act of Parliament to deal with the climatic consequences of fossil fuel burning – an Act that was to lead to the run-down of coal as our principal energy source.

London, as the largest city in Britain, consumed the most coal to meet its energy requirements. It was not however, conveniently close to the major coal mining areas. After the Great Fire of London in 1666, the government had brought in laws to encourage coal to be burnt to reduce the risk of wood fire sparks. The Industrial

Revolution triggered a greatly increased demand. By the 1840s there were some 580 collier brigs bringing coal from such ports as Blyth, South Shields, Sunderland and Hartlepool. But there were many losses of both ships and men, due not only due to weather conditions, but also due to unseaworthy craft overloaded by unscrupulous owners. In 1868, the coal merchant Samuel Plimsoll became a Liberal MP, and despite opposition from shipowners, he eventually succeeded in introducing the Plimsoll line to denote the safe loading level on ships.

The early steam bulk carriers were largely pioneered in the London coal trade in the 1840s. The screw steamer *John Bowes*, built at Jarrow in 1852, was the first successful steam collier and the precurser of many others.

In 1792 William Murdock became the first person to make practical use of gas for lighting his home in Cornwall. The first public display of gas lighting took place in 1807 when Frederick Winsor gave a display of lighting in Pall Mall to celebrate the birthday of the Prince of Wales. The manufacture of coal gas for public use began in England when the Gas Light and Coke Company was founded in 1812. It gained a Royal Charter authorising the installation of a 21-year supply of gas to the Cities of London and Westminster and the Borough of Southwark. A first gasworks was built at Great Peter Street in Westminster in 1812, which by 1822 was processing 10,000 tons of coal a year. Soon there was a proliferation of local gas companies making or supplying gas. The coal for these local gasworks, to meet the needs of a rapidly growing London, was brought either by rail or by sea. While electricity would eventually become the norm for lighting, when it came to cooking it was estimated that by 1939 there were eight or nine gas cookers for every electric cooker in use.

Beckton gasworks was the biggest in the world. Started in 1868 and opened by the Gas Light & Coke Company (GL&CC) in 1870, when fully developed it covered an area larger than the 'square mile' of the City of London. It was named after the first Governor Simon Adams Beck. The coal was delivered by ship and unloaded by hydraulic cranes to be conveyed to the retort houses. The works had an extensive internal railway network serving both the retort houses and the by-products plants. This even featured a roundhouse engine shed. It was worked by a number of 0-4-0 tank locos in green livery for the main works, red for the by-products plant. These were of cut-down design because of low clearances. The GL&CC amalgamated with some of its less efficient rivals such as the Imperial Company who had works at Bromley-by-Bow. By 1945 it accounted for 12 per cent of total national gas sales. Following nationalisation of the gas industry in 1948–9, Beckton came under the ownership of North Thames Gas.

With the development of railways, much of the coal for household use, and for those local electricity power stations and gasworks that were built without river or canal access, was brought to London in trains of loose coupled, unfitted wooden (later steel) mineral wagons which were trundled slowly to the main marshalling yards, such as Ferme Park or Brent, where they would be split up into trains for delivery to local station goods yards. From here household coal would be delivered in sacks to the door by local coal merchants.

As gas, and later electricity became increasingly used, the tonnage of coal required by the gasworks and power stations was such that it could not be realistically carried entirely by rail. Some three-quarters of the total coal supplied to London (up to 13m tons) still came by sea. Coal was shipped to power stations located on the Thames. These included Woolwich, Greenwich, Deptford, Bankside 'A', and most famous of them all, Battersea power station, all on the south side of the river. In the late 1940s, some four million tons a year was shipped from the northeast, principally from Blyth and Jarrow where the coal was tipped directly into the colliers from rail-served staithes. To give some idea of the tonnage consumed, Woolwich Power Station alone would burn over 1,000 tons a day when working at its peak.

Battersea was built for the London Power Company, designed by the celebrated architect Sir Giles Gilbert Scott. When it opened in 1931, it was regarded as the most advanced generator in Europe. Its chimneys were fitted with sulphur extractors to reduce pollution. Originally there were two 300ft high chimneys, but it was doubled in size in 1948 and the extra two chimneys added to produce the outline familiar to Londoners today.

Greenwich power station predated the First World War, having been built by the London County Council in 1906 to provide power for its electric tramways. Ownership passed to London Transport in 1933. After the trams went in 1952, and trolleybuses in 1962, Greenwich became a backup to Lots Road, providing power for the Underground.

Lots Road power station, on the north bank of the Thames at Chelsea was started in 1902 and opened in 1905. It was built to provide power for the District Railway (now District Line), which was being electrified. The site was chosen because of easy supply of coal by barges and a ready supply of cooling water. When opened it was said to be the largest generating station in the world. Its thirty-two boilers provided steam to turn the eight generators which supplied current at 11,000 volts ac, which was then converted at substations to 550–600 volts dc for the company's lines. They burned around 6,100 tonnes of small grained 'pea' coal a week. The power station was far larger than would be needed just for the District Railway, but the Chairman, Charles Tyson Yerkes had expansionist plans. He had offered to pay for the electrification of the lines of the District's great rival, the Metropolitan Railway in return for a royalty payment or to run the Metropolitan for their shareholders in return for a higher dividend than they were currently receiving. The Metropolitan board turned him down and built their own rail-served power station at Neasden. Both were to pass to London Transport in 1933.

The Electricity Supply Act of 1926 set up the Central Electricity Board, which set standards and established the National Grid. In 1948, electricity supply was nationalised, with the power stations becoming the responsibility of the Central Electricity Generating Board. At first, they chartered fifty colliers to deliver their supplies, with much of the management undertaken by the established firm of Stephenson Clarke. But from 1950, they started to purchase their own vessels. Most of these were fitted with steam reciprocating engines. At first these were coal burning, to take advantage of the ready supply of coal at the ports of loading. However, after 1954, oil burning was specified. By 1965, they had a fleet of twenty-nine colliers, dating from between 1939–1955, of which twenty-one were steam powered.

Delivery to the power stations and gas works upriver beyond London Bridge, such as Battersea, required specially built vessels with low superstructures, lowering funnels and telescopic masts that could pass under the bridges. These were nicknamed 'flatirons' and could reach upriver as far as Wandsworth gas works, which had an annual intake of around 500,000 tons. The first of these 'flatirons' had been the *Vauxhall*, *Westminster* and *Lambeth*, built in 1878. Typical of the post-war period was the *Wimbledon* of 1931, which could carry around 2,400 tons of coal; and the CEGB's *Hackney* built in 1962.

In the early 1960s there was a total of thirty-nine gas or electricity generating stations along the River Thames.

With so many chimneys belching out smoke from burning coal there was an effect on the climate. This had been noted in London as early as the seventeenth century. John Evelyn in his *Fumifugium* (1661) wrote of 'that hellish and dismall cloud of sea-coale'. From Victorian times London was increasingly plagued by dense fogs known as 'London peculiars' or 'peasoupers'. These were conditions of smog, a term coined in 1905 by Dr H. A. Des Voeux, and occurring in particular meteorological conditions in which smoke particles from the domestic and industrial burning of coal become trapped in fog.

On 4 December 1952 an anticyclone settled over London. The sky was clear, and it was colder than usual, as it had been for some weeks, so there were plenty of fires burning. The wind dropped and the air near the ground was moist. Conditions were ideal for the formation of smog.

During the day of 5 December, the fog was not particularly dense, although it had a dry, smoky character. However, when nightfall came, the fog thickened and visibility fell to a few metres. It then stayed at below 50 metres continuously for the next 48 hours, and below 500 metres for 114 hours until 10 December. Road, rail and air transport were brought to a standstill. Even theatres had to close as fog in the auditoriums made conditions intolerable. Finally, winds from the west blew the fog away down the Thames Estuary and out into the North Sea.

But it was not just disruption to work and transport that resulted from the smog. Lives were lost. The previous week the death rate had been 2,062, close to normal for that time of year. The following week 4,703 people died, with a peak on the 8 and 9 December of 900 a day. In parts of the East End, death rates during the smog were nine times the normal. The death rate remained above normal throughout the winter and into the following spring. Official figures show some 4,000 people died prematurely during the smog and the two weeks after. The death rate then returned to normal for a short while, but this may have been due to registrations being delayed by the Christmas holidays. For after Christmas deaths then returned to a higher than normal rate for some time. Although the true figure may never be known, it is reckoned that up to 12,000 people died as a result of the Great London Smog.

With graphs showing the correlation between the death rate and the intensity of smoke and sulphur dioxide pollution levels, something had to be done. Following the report of the Beaver Committee the first Clean Air Act was introduced in 1956. This aimed to control domestic sources of smoke pollution by introducing smokeless zones. In these areas, smokeless fuels had to be burnt. These cleaner fuels reduced both smoke and sulphur dioxide levels. New power stations were to be built away from major cities, preferably closer to coalfields. Tall chimney stacks on power stations would help disperse the air pollution caused.

Parts of London, Manchester, Salford and Bolton were early places to be declared as smokeless zones. Some emissions would still be allowed, but householders were offered grants towards the cost of converting coal-burning grates to smokeless fuel.

With the Act in force, there came changes to the pattern of power supply. More oil, gas, and nuclear-powered power stations began to appear. Many new coal-fired power stations such as Drax and West Burton were built, sited near the main coalfields, supplied by 'merry-go-round' trains. Within London, the rail-served and the older upriver Thames-side coal-fired power stations eventually closed. New coal-fired stations were built further down river at West Thurrock (1954), Tilbury 'A' (1958) and 'B' (1965) and Littlebrook (1983). Three 19,000-ton diesel colliers were ordered to supply these. Other power stations were built on the River Medway, such as Kingsnorth. By 1974 CEGB's fleet had shrunk to four steam and six diesel ships. The oldest and last coal burning collier was the 3,345-ton *Cliffe Quay*, built by Wm. Pickersgill at Sunderland in 1950. She brought coal to London or to the Ipswich power station that she was named after (itself now closed). When the oil-fired *James Rowan*, built 1955, 2,947 tons gross was withdrawn and broken up in 1984, she was the last steam collier to trade under the British flag.

Woolwich Power Station was demolished in 1979 and the site is now redeveloped. The jetty, stripped of its equipment, remains in the river. Coal-fired Bankside 'A' closed in 1959. Oil-fired Bankside 'B', opened in 1947, was closed in 1981 and has been transformed into the Tate Modern art gallery. At Battersea, the shell of the building, a listed structure, stood derelict since closure in 1983 as successive plans for its redevelopment as a leisure complex etc failed to materialise. Only in 2014 did redevelopment start and this is ongoing. On the river, the jetty remains, its cranes intact and forlornly waiting for the next shipment of coal that will never come.

The newer power stations remained in use for longer but these have now closed and been demolished. Tilbury received regular coal supplies until 2011, but the fuel was imported from such sources as Poland or the Baltic states, and latterly came in vessels of up to 70,000 tons or so. From May 2011 work began to convert Tilbury B to run on biomass wood pellets. However, on 27 February 2012 a major fire broke out in a fuel storage area. Following this, in 2013 the owners RWE npower announced that they were ceasing conversion. The power station was decommissioned and has since been demolished. Kingsnorth power station on the Medway, latterly operated by E-On (formerly Powergen) was supplied by the British colliers *Sir Charles Parsons* and *Lord Hinton* built in 1985/6, c.22,000 tons.

The Underground and British Railways coal fired power stations have also closed. Neasden closed in 1968 and has been demolished. Lots Road was converted to oil-burning in the 1960s. It finally closed in October 2002, since when the Underground has been fully supplied with electricity from the National Grid, as have the former BR lines. Greenwich was fitted with gas turbine generators in 1972 and remains in use as an emergency back-up supply in case of Grid failure.

In 1965–6 vast resources of natural gas were discovered beneath the North Sea in British waters. This gas was 'clean', burning without giving rise to pollution from smoke, soot and sulphur dioxide, and so readily compliant with the Clean Air Act requirements. Within 18 months a tenth of Britain's gas needs were being met by North Sea gas, with a mass programme to convert domestic appliances across the country. It spelt the end for coal gas production. Beckton closed down in 1969. The spoil tips, nicknamed the 'Beckton Alps', were landscaped and turned into a ski slope. The whole works buildings were contaminated and thus unsuited for housing development. The dilapidated buildings were notably used as a setting for the film *Full Metal Jacket* where they represented the aftermath of war damage in Vietnam. Clearance and redevelopment into a retail park did not take place until the 1990s. The disused jetty still remains *in situ*, having defied all attempts to demolish it.

Another Thameside gas works was the South Metropolitan's 150-acre plant at East Greenwich. Here, gas was latterly produced by converting liquid methane imported from Africa. After closure and demolition, the site became home to the Millennium Dome.

Ironically perhaps, North Sea gas is now running out, and Britain is importing liquefied natural gas (LNG) to meet peak demand. Like the coal before it, this is coming by sea, in specially designed tankers from such countries as Algeria. A dedicated terminal opened on the Isle of Grain on the River Medway in 2004 and receives regular shipments.

SS *Cliffe Quay* (1950, 3,345grt) was the last coal-fired steam collier owned by the CEGB. She is seen near Beckton in July 1977.

Another of the CEGB steam driven colliers was the *Sir John Snell* (1955, 2,947grt), built by Hall Russell & Co Ltd, Aberdeen.

A sister ship to the *Sir John Snell*, the CEGB owned *James Rowan* (1955, 2,947grt) was the last steam collier to trade under the British flag. She is seen here passing Gravesend in July 1979.

Stephenson Clarke Ltd *Shoreham* (1957, 1,834grt), 1977.

Rather more modern was Stephenson Clarke Ltd *Dallington* (1975, 7,658grt), 1979.

Sumburgh Head (1977, 4,694grt) was a collier owned by Christian Salvesen and was on charter to the CEGB. Taken in 1979.

A typical 'flatiron', the *Tarring* (1958, 1,877grt) shows the low superstructure layout which enabled these ships to pass under the central London bridges to reach power stations such as Battersea. The masts were of necessity telescopic. She was owned by Stephenson Clarke, and was seen in Gallions Reach in 1977. She was ex South Eastern Gas Board's *Lambeth* in 1970.

CEGB owned *Harry Richardson* (1950, 1,777grt) seen in 1977.

Woolwich Power station in 1975. The chimney nearest the river was removed by 1977 and the whole site demolished in 1979.

The iconic shape of Battersea Power station, derelict in 2013, before redevelopment started. *Photo by Malcolm Batten.*

Container ships

The *Jervis Bay* (1970, 26,876grt) of OCL arrives at Tilbury in 1978. It was this ship that initiated OCL container services from Tilbury in May 1970. There were six ships in this series including *Flinders Bay* (1969, 26,756 grt), all having this unusual funnel design.

A later OCL ship *Mairangi Bay* (1978, 43,995grt). This next generation of container ship was considerably larger than its predecessors.

OCL *Resolution Bay* (1977, 43,995grt) in 1979.

OCL *Largs Bay* (1977, 52,007grt) seen from the Gravesend side in 1981.

Associated Container Transportation Ltd was a consortium formed of Ben Line, Blue Star Line, Cunard, Ellerman Lines, T & J Harrison and Port Line for container services to Australia from 1969. This is their *ACT 7* (1977, 43,992grt) in 1980. Again this shows the growth in size of container ships – *ACT 5* built in 1972 had been 24,212grt carrying c.1,300 TEU (twenty foot equivalent units).

Australian National Line *Australian Venture* (1977, 43,878grt), 1982.

On charter to Canadian Pacific (CP Ships) in 1981 was the German owned *CP Hunter* (1980, 16,230grt), originally the *Pamina*.

South African Marine Corporation (Safmarine) *S. A. Sederberg* (1978, 52,615grt) in 1981. One of four sister ships known as 'Big Whites', she, along with *S. A. Helderberg, S. A. Waterberg* and *S. A. Winterberg* had a capacity of 2,464 TEU.

On charter to the United Arab Maritime Company in 1982 was the *Ibn Al Akfani* (1981, 17,519grt). The owners were Horst-Werner Janssen of Germany.

Lloyd Triestino, Italy *Lloydiana* (1972, 28,688grt), 1978.

Royal Nedlloyd Group *Nedlloyd Tasman* (1971, 27,614grt) previously the *Abel Tasman* until 1978. Photographed in 1982.

Combi-carrier *Mentor* (1980, 16,482grt) working on charter to Elder Dempster in 1981. Seven of this type were built, four in Japan and three on the Clyde. Some worked on charter to OCL such as the *Maron*, renamed as *Studland Bay*, and these also visited Tilbury.

Container feeder ships

Bell Lines *Bell Ranger* (1976, 1,598grt) taken in 1977. Bell Lines ran from Victoria Deep Wharf container terminal from 1976 with a service to Rotterdam.

Prince Line *Sailor Prince* (1971, 1,599 grt), 1976.

Prince Line *Crown Prince* (1979, 1,599grt), anchored off Gravesend, 1980.

Ellerman City Liners *City of Florence* (1970, 1,599 grt) ex *Tua* in 1974. Seen in 1981.

Mauricio di Oliveira (1970, 2,912grt) was owned by Cia Portuguesa de Transportes. Seen passing Woolwich in 1976.

Dutch *Yolanda* (1978, 997grt) owned by Comar Scheepvaart. 1979.

Russian owned Rinella Line *Kapitan Tomson* (1977, 4,627grt) ex *RS Ixion,* 1981.

Bugsier Line *Weser* (1974, 999grt), 1980.

Cuxhaven (1976, 999grt) was German owned by Hans-Rainer Numssen. 1979.

Deutsche Nah-Ost Line, Germany, *Karvatein* (1980, 3,348grt), 1981.

The Hellenic Line were chartering the *Esteclipper* (1980, 3,052grt) from owners Gerd Ritscher of Germany, 1981.

Walter Bartels, Germany, *Nincop II* (1977, 1,599grt), 1979.

Container/Ro-Ro

These vessels combined two of the latest technologies with capacity to load both containers and also vehicles via the stern ramp. Grimaldi Lines of Italy are regular visitors to Tilbury in 2020 with such ships, berthing at both the Northfleet Hope container terminal and the Ro-Ro terminal in turn.

Renoir (1973, 13928 tons) was owned by Compagnie Generale Maritimes (CGM) along with the *Cezanne, Gauguin* and *Degas*. 1979.

Also owned was the *Monet* (1978, 13,928grt), seen in 1979.

Wilhelmsen, Norway were owners of *Tricolor* (1972, 23,912grt), seen here in 1981.

Dredgers

Dredgers continue to be daily visitors to various private wharves along the Thames. They bring in sea-dredged aggregates for building work from controlled dredging grounds in the North Sea and off the south coast.

Murphy & Sons' steam dredger *Ebbw* (1948, 823grt) passing Woolwich in the 1960s.

ARC Marine Ltd *Arco Severn* (1974, 1,599grt), 1977.

South Coast Shipping Co. *Sand Weaver* (1975, 3,366grt), 1982.

Civil & Marine Ltd *Cambrae* (1973, 3,896grt), 1981.

Civil & Marine Ltd *Cambourne* (1980, 3,182grt) 1982. She later became the *Arco Bourne* when ARC Marine took over Civil & Marine in 1995.

Westminster Dredging *Nabstone* (1970,1,579grt) ex *Chichester Gem*, 1979.

Norwest Sand & Gravel Co Ltd *Norleader* (1967, 1,590grt), 1977.

British Dredging *Bowknight* (1974, 2,965grt), 1977.

Adriaan Volker (Holland) *Geopotes VI* (1963, 5,146grt), 1980.

The PLA was responsible for dredging the river to maintain adequate draught for shipping, including at riverside wharves. Around 1980 the Tate & Lyle refinery wharf was suffering from silt build-up making berthing difficult for ships bringing in the raw cane sugar. However, the PLA was reluctant to get involved as it was closing the local docks and concentrating resources on Tilbury. Tate & Lyle approached the local shipbuilders, Cubow at Woolwich, who at the time were building coastal tankers for Bowker & King Ltd to see if they could design and build a small self-propelling suction dredger. This was the resulting vessel.

Roll-on, Roll-off ships

The use of these grew increasingly common during the 1970s, predominantly by Scandinavian operators bringing in forest products (newsprint etc). All these views are at Tilbury. Note that many of these are also carrying containers.

The United Baltic Corporation ran a weekly service from Purfleet Deep Wharf to Rotterdam and Helsinki. *Baltic Progess* (1974, 4,668grt) is inbound in 1981. Her sister ship was *Baltic Eagle*.

Finncarriers *Orion* (1973, 4,469grt) 1980.

Lundqvist (United Lines), Finland, *Gunilla* (1972, 2,385grt).

Eimskip, Iceland, *Eyrarfoss* (1978, 1,599grt) ex *Mercandian Importer II* 1982. Note how the containers have been stacked!

Gorthon Lines, Sweden, *Lovisa Gorthon* (1979, 4,094grt).

Lennart Kihlberg (Holmen Carrier), Sweden, *Bravik* (1974, 1,599grt), 1977.

Brostroms Rederi, Sweden, *Timmerland* (1978, 9,350grt) 1979.

Uglands Rederi, Norway, *Ugland Carrier* built in 1978. Shown in 1982.

Sealink Rederi, Sweden, *Nordic Link* (1981, 5,006grt), 1981. The design is perhaps described as functional rather than graceful.

Polish owned *Inowroclaw* (1980, 7,510grt) maintained a weekly service from Tilbury to Gdynia. She could carry cars and containers and had accommodation for twelve passengers. 1980.

Interroll SA, Spain, *Carinigo* (1981, 1,464grt) with a cargo of cars in 1982. A predecessor to modern vehicle carriers.

Sludge carriers

When London's sewage was treated at the outfall stations at Barking Creek and Crossness, a quantity of sewage sludge was produced. This was loaded into specially designed vessels which took it out 55 miles to the Black Deep in the Thames Estuary on the ebb tide and then dumped it in slack water. Five vessels were employed on this work. On 18 September 1965 one such boat, the *Sir Joseph Rawlinson*, was involved in a collision in the estuary and sank with loss of life. Sewage dumping ended at the end of 1998 owing to new EC regulations and now sewage sludge is burned in incinerators at Beckton and Crossness.

The Greater London Council's *Hounslow*, built in 1968 returns to its base at Beckton after discharging sludge in May 1979. These sludge boats were nicknamed 'Bovril boats'.

GLC *Newham* (1966, 2,175grt) 1980.

Sir Joseph Bazalgette (1963, 2,258grt) 1981.

Last of the GLC sludge boats *Thames* (1977, 2,663grt) in 1978. When the GLC was abolished in 1986 these ships passed to the Thames Water Authority.

Special purpose ships

Lykes Bros Steamship Co. Inc. had three barge-carrying vessels: *Almeira Lykes*, *Doctor Lykes* and *Tillie Lykes* (all 1972, 21,667grt). This is a stern view of *Doctor Lykes* showing the barge entrance. They would moor in the river at Gravesend between the piers on their trips from the US Gulf ports.

Tillie Lykes in 1981. A tug is alongside with one of the 'Seabee' barges laden with containers. This system was known as LASH (Lighter Aboard SHip).

Tillie Lykes arriving at Tilbury in 1979. In the winter of 1985–6 the trio were sold to the US Military Sea Lift Command.

Cable ship *John W. MacKay* at AEI Cables, Enderby Wharf, Greenwich. To the right of the ship can be seen the container crane of the Victoria Deep Water Terminal Ltd – one of the upriver facilities used by container feeder ships rather than Tilbury Dock or Northfleet Hope.

Cable ship *John W. MacKay* in 1981. Owned by the Commercial Cable Co. this steam reciprocating powered veteran dated from 1922. After withdrawal she spent a period laid up in Portsmouth Harbour for a failed attempt at preservation before she was towed to Turkey for scrapping in 1994.

Cable & Wireless Ltd owned the *Mercury* cable ship (1962, 8,962 grt) passing Woolwich power station in the 1960s. She was built by Cammell Laird, Birkenhead.

London & Rochester Trading Co. cable coaster *Gardience* (1969, 424grt), 1979.

Mammoet heavy lift ship *Happy Rider* (1976, 1,599grt) 1978.

Marinus Smits, Holland, heavy lift ship *Alida Smits* (1978, 3,544grt) 1978.

Heavy lift ship *Marinus Smits* (1976, 1,600grt), 1977.

The heavy lift ship *Aberthaw Fisher* was owned by the CEGB but managed by Fisher. In 1979 she arrived at Tilbury Docks to load transformers for Hamburg.

Tankers

Tankers would bring crude oil to the refineries at Shell Haven and Coryton, both now closed, but they did not proceed as far as Tilbury. However, other tankers would come to discharge at oil terminals around Purfleet and Dagenham. There were also smaller vessels that came right up through central London to serve terminals and also to provide bunkering for the tugs and pleasure craft based there.

British Petroleum *British Tamar* (1973, 15,644grt) 1978.

Esso owned *Esso Albany* (1973, 12,800grt) 1982.

Shell UK Ltd *Shell Director* (1972, 1,210grt) ex *Caernarvon*, 1982.

Shell UK Ltd *Shell Trader* (1966, 1,177grt).

Texaco Inc.*Texaco Rotterdam* (1968, 14,948grt) 1978.

Carl Buttner, Germany, *Butt* (1980,6,355grt) This was new at the time when seen being berthed at Purfleet in 1980.

By contrast, dating from 1960 is *Finale* (22,424grt). Owned by Transmarina of Italy she had previously been *Bergemaster* of Bergesen. Shown in 1979.

Also dating from 1960, *Uje* was owned by the Swiss company World Shipping. At 11,778grt she had been Shell's *Amoria* until 1979. Shown in 1982.

Palva (1964, 11,136grt) owned by Neste O/Y of Finland.

Russian owned *Linkuva* (1980, 4,816grt).

Christopher Rowbotham & Sons Ltd *Stellaman* (1976, 1,513grt) 1982.

Stephenson Clarke Ltd *Maplehurst* (1961, 1,760grt), 1978.

A line up including F. T. Everard's *Alacrity* (1966, 943grt) and *Authority* (1966, 499grt) in 1981.

Leth & Co *Ludwig* (1969, 1,208grt) 1980.

Coastal tanker *Nicholas M* (1965, 1.308grt) had been owned by Metcalf Motor Coasters but was now owned by Coe Metcalf Shipping, as was the coaster *Firethorn*, 1981. (see p. 37)

J. P. Knight coastal tanker *Kingsthorpe* (1956, 303grt). She had been the Shell-Mex & BP *BP Manufacturer* until 1969.

Vinalmar SA (Switzerland) *Rhone* (1974, 1,599grt), a specialised wine tanker. 1978.

Another wine tanker was the *Astree* (1954, 3,055grt) owned by Soc. Navale Caennaise of France. Seen in 1977. From 1976 all bulk wine was handled at the India and Millwall Docks, much having earlier been handled at London Docks.

Tankers – upriver

Bowker & King Ltd *Beechcroft* (1966, 540grt) 1981.

Shell-Mex & BP Ltd coastal tanker *Pronto* (1967, 652grt) approaches Chelsea Bridge on 10 November 1974. The masts are folded down for clearance under the bridges. *Photo by Malcolm Batten.*

The same vessel, now renamed as *BP Alert,* passes Tilbury in 1980 with masts erected.

Shell-Mex & BP Ltd coastal tanker *Perfecto* (1967, 500grt) passes under Grosvenor Bridge, Chelsea, which takes the railway line into Victoria Station. 12 October 1977. *Photo by Malcolm Batten.*

Tugs – lighterage and launch tugs

In the 1960s there were some 7,000 lighters within the docks, on the river, and in its tributaries. About 350 lighterage tugs distributed some 60 per cent of the cargo passing through the port. Tugs were allowed to tow a maximum of six lighters at a time. There were several companies, and some tugs were veterans, albeit much rebuilt. Smaller launch tugs or 'toshers' could work in the more confined spaces to position lighters.

Tug *Britannia* at the entrance to the KGV lock, 1977. In the 1970s she was the oldest working tug on the Thames. She had been built in 1893 for the South Metropolitan Gas Co. as a steam tug. Conversion to diesel came in 1955. Owners were the Greenhithe Lighterage Co. Ltd.

J. P. Knight Ltd, Rochester merged with Gaselee & Son Ltd in 1966 to form Gaselee & Knight Ltd. This is the *Khurdah* (1930, 50grt) with Knight's funnel markings.

F. T. Everard & Sons Ltd *R. A. Everard* (1943, 87grt) at Woolwich in 1979. She had been built as the *Pinklake* for the River Lighterage Co. Ltd, passing to W. E. White & Sons in 1960 and to F. T. Everard & Sons Ltd a year later. They converted her from steam to diesel in 1962.

The tug *Knocker White* (1924, 96grt) was built in Holland as the *Cairnrock* for Harrisons Lighterage Co. London. She later passed to W. E. White & Sons, Rotherhithe and was renamed. Converted to diesel in 1960, she was here seen by the Woolwich ferry in 1980. In front of her is the smaller *Sarah White* (1925, 30grt). She was sold for scrap in 1982 but became part of the Museum of London collection in 1984 with the help of a grant from the LDDC. After the Museum of London Docklands opened in 2003 *Knocker White* was moored outside in West India Dock, although she has since been moved.

W. E. White & Sons' *Boys White* (1956, 58grt) Woolwich ex *Falconbrook.* 1979.

Thames & General Lighterage Ltd *General IX* and Cory tug *Touchstone* (1962, 75grt) Tilbury 1979. Thames & General were taken over by William Cory & Son (Cory Lighterage) in 1980.

Crew and a diver aboard the *General IX* tug at Gravesend. The 'T' on the funnel indicates that this is one of the Thames & General Lighterage Ltd fleet.

Two unidentified tugs seen from above, c.1949.

Darling Bros *Arthur Darling* (1946, 50grt) was ex John Hawkins Ltd *John Hawkins* in 1969. Taken 1976. She was sold a year later.

Unico dated from 1927 when she was built for the Union Lighterage Co. Ltd. In 1971 she passed to J. T. Palmer & Sons, Gravesend and remained in service until broken up in 2013. At Tilbury in 1980.

London & Rochester Trading Co. Ltd completed a pair of pusher tugs at Strood, the *Lashette* in 1971 for themselves and *Grey Lash* in 1978 for Humphrey & Grey (Lighterage) Ltd. These were to work barges for the LASH (Lighter Aboard SHip) vessels. In 1983 *Grey Lash* also passed to London & Rochester Trading and was renamed *Shovette*.

River Lighterage *Tyburn Brook* (1950, 70grt) photographed from Waterloo bridge. Moored at the Embankment can be seen a range of heritage shipping. Nearest is the *Discovery* (1901), the first British ship to be built for scientific exploration, and used by Captain Scott for his Antarctic voyages between 1901–4. She was acquired by the Maritime Trust in 1979 and moved into St Katherine's Dock. However, in 1986 she was returned to Dundee where she was built. Also seen are HMS *Wellington,* built in 1934, *President* (originally *Saxifrage*), and *Crysanthemum*. The latter are survivors of the 72-strong 'Flower' class built for the Royal Navy during the First World War as 'Q' ships or decoy ships to provide armed escort for convoys against German U-boats.

Humphrey & Grey (Lighterage) Ltd *Friston Down* (1964, 99grt) approaches Hungerford Bridge. She was built by Richard Dunston Ltd. Former River Clyde paddle steamer *Old Caledonia* can be seen by Waterloo Bridge on 23 October 1973. In 1983 *Friston Down* was sold to London & Rochester Trading Co. Ltd and in 2013 passed to GPS Marine as *GPS Anglia*. Photo by Malcolm Batten.

Until 1985 domestic rubbish for landfill was not containerised but put into lighters and covered by a tarpaulin. William Cory & Sons Ltd tug *Recruit* (1952, 91grt) marshals lighters at the City of Westminster's Gatliff Road Wharf near Grosvenor Bridge on 10 October 1977. They would then be taken to Mucking or Rainham Marshes. From 1985 new barges were provided to take the rubbish in containers from the various loading points. Their successors, Cory Environmental, still take these containers, but since 2011 the rubbish goes for incineration at the Riverside Resource Recovery Facility at Belvedere. *Recruit* still survives, albeit much rebuilt, with GPS Marine as the *GPS Cervia*. Photo by Malcolm Batten.

Cory Tank Lighterage Ltd *Swiftstone* (1952, 91grt) brings domestic rubbish lighters under Grosvenor Bridge carrying the railway line out of Victoria station. *Swiftstone* was a sister ship to the *Recruit*, both being built by Richard Dunston Ltd. *Photo by Malcolm Batten.*

Associated Portland Cement Manufacturers Ltd *Cemenco* (1948, 116grt) near Chelsea Bridge 10 October 1977. *Photo by Malcolm Batten.*

Commercial lighter traffic used to extend right up the tidal Thames. Here in the 1940s a steam tug is seen with a pair of loaded lighters at Hampton Court. The name is partly obscured but is possibly *Pamela Alice*.

Mercantile Lighterage Ltd was a subsidiary of William Cory & Son Ltd. This is their launch tug *Merano* at Woolwich, 1979.

Thames & General Lighterage Ltd launch tug *Eager*, KGV lock 1979.

Cloudy (1948) was the first of four launch tugs built at Wivenhoe for James W. Cook & Co, London between 1948 and 1952. They were taken over by Cory Lighterage in 1958 and placed in their subsidiary Mercantile Lighterage fleet. Shown in 1977.

Launch tug *Leonie* in KGV Dock, 1979.

Launch tug *Nipalong* at Tilbury. Owned by J. T. Palmer & Sons of Gravesend. This company's fleet also included tugs *Niparound* and *Nipaway*.

In 1951 the PLA received three small launch tugs built by James Pollock Sons & Co. Ltd. These were the *Placate* and the slightly smaller *Plashy* and *Plaudit*. The last of these is seen here at the entrance to KGV in 1980.

SERVICE VESSELS

Tugs – ship handling

The Port of London Authority had its own tugs working within the enclosed docks. In the 1930s, six other firms were involved in ship towage. By 1968 this was down to two, and then in January 1969 W. H. J. Alexander Ltd (Sun Tugs) merged with Ship Towage (London) Ltd to form London Tugs Ltd with thirty-six tugs at formation. This merger, and the rundown and closure of the inner docks from 1968 led to a rapid clear-out of the older tugs. On 1 January 1975 the Alexandra Towing Co. Ltd of Liverpool took over the operations of London Tugs Ltd to form Alexandra Towing Co. (London) with a fleet of twenty-three tugs.

The PLA had its own fleet of tugs for manoeuvring ships within the Royal Docks. This is the *Plangent*, built in 1951. She worked for the PLA until 1986, when she was sold to new owners in Greece. Taken in 1975. Other PLA tugs dating from this period were the *Plagel*, *Plateau* and *Platina*.

Plangent (1951, 159grt) takes the pull as she brings a vessel from the entrance lock into King George V dock in 1975. Built by Scarrs of Hessle.

The last four ship-handling tugs for the PLA were a quartet from Richard Dunston Ltd, Hessle, in 1965/6. These were the *Plasma, Platoon, Plankton* and *Placard*. They had Voith Schneider propulsion units. *Plankton* is seen here in 1977. After the PLA sold Tilbury docks in 1991, *Plasma* and *Platoon* were sold to Alexandra Towing as *Burma* and *Dhulia*, while *Placard* and *Plankton* passed to the new Port of Tilbury Ltd and became *Orsett* and *Linford*.

A contemporary advert for W. H. J. Alexander 'Sun Tugs' from the PLA directory 1963.

W. H. J. Alexander Ltd steam tug *Sun XV* (1925, 183grt) seen at Woolwich in 1949. She was withdrawn in the big clear-out of 1969, along with *Sun VIII* (1919), *Sun X* (1920) and *Sun XII* (1925).

Sun XXIII (1961, 150grt) in 1979. Built by Philip & Son Ltd at Dartmouth, she was sold in 1984, only to come back to the Thames as the *Suncrest* for S&H Towage in 1985.

Sun XXIV (1962, 120grt) at Woolwich in 1976. She was transferred to Southampton in 1979. As with most of the other tugs seen in these pages she carries the funnel colours of Alexandra Towing Co.

Sun tugs at base in 1975. *Sun II* (1965, 150grt) was built by Charles D. Holmes, Hull for use at the West India and Royal Docks, and remained on the Thames until sold in 1992. She is seen here with *Sun XXIV*.

The first new tugs for Alexandra Towing Co.'s Thames fleet were three ordered from Richard Dunston Ltd, Hessle, for delivery in 1977. *Sun Kent* (1977, 292grt) had a controllable-pitch propeller in a steerable Kort nozzle and was equipped for firefighting. *Sun Essex* was similar.

The third of the trio was *Sun London,* which differed in not being equipped for firefighting.

Steam tug *Cervia*, 233 tons gross, was built for the British Government as the *Empire Raymond* in 1946 by Alexander Hall & Co. Ltd, Aberdeen. She was acquired by William Watkins Ltd and renamed in 1947. She passed to Ship Towage (London) Ltd and then to London Tugs Ltd in 1969. Taken at the entrance to the Royal Docks in August 1949, she is escorting Glen Lines *Glenearn* (1938, 8,888grt) from the lock ready for departure down river. She was withdrawn from service in 1972 and subsequently sold to the East Kent Maritime Trust in 1985.

Burma (1966, 165grt) was also acquired by London Tugs Ltd from William Watkins Ltd in 1969. When built she surprisingly had an open wheelhouse of pre-war appearance, but this was later enclosed. Shown here in 1977.

Dhulia (1959, 272grt), another of the former William Watkins Ltd tugs. She was built by Henry Scarr Ltd, Hessle. William Watkins Ltd was one of the earliest tug companies being established in 1833. It merged with Elliott Steam Tugs and Gamecock Tugs to form Ship Towage (London) in 1950. The tugs continued to wear the funnel colours of their previous owners.

Moorcock (1959, 273grt), originally supplied in Gamecock Tugs colours, was a sister ship to the *Dhulia*. Both had a limited fire-fighting capability. She was scrapped in 1982. Taken in 1979.

Vanquisher (1955, 294grt) was built for the Elliott Steam Tug Co. Ltd. fleet of Ship Towage (London) Ltd. At the time she was the most powerful single-screw tug on the Thames. In 1965 ownership passed to William Watkins Ltd and then in turn to Ship Towage Ltd. She was finally withdrawn for breaking in 1982. This view is from 1979.

Vanquisher seen passing Woolwich in the 1960s with London Tugs Ltd funnel markings. In January 1986 she capsized after being pulled over by the tow rope from OCL's container ship *Jervis Bay*. No lives were lost and the tug later returned to service.

Avenger and *Hibernia* were a pair of fire-fighting equipped tugs supplied by Cochrane & Sons Ltd, Selby, to Ship Towage (London) Ltd in 1963. They were upgraded with a controllable-pitch propeller in 1974/5 and remained in service until 1985 and 1987 respectively. *Avenger* was then sold to Canadian owners and *Hibernia* went to Greece. *Hibernia* is seen in 1977.

Alexandra Towing Co. *Waterloo* (1977, 315grt) is taking the strain as the stern tug for a ship at Tilbury.

Tugs at Gravesend line up at Denton moorings, Gravesend. One of the PLA salvage vessels can also be seen.

An attempt to compete with the existing ship handling tug companies mounted by Reef Tugs proved to be short-lived when their first customer was blockaded in Tilbury by seven local tugs. The chartered *Daunt Reef* (1958, 160grt) is moored up out of use in 1981. She was owned by Hapag and previously named *Centaur*.

Smit Internationale, Holland, ocean going tug *Hudson* (1964, 670grt,) 1976.

Port services

PLA launch *Sea Cutter,* 1978.

A PLA driftwood boat, 1977.

PLA dredger *Gallions Reach* operating at the entrance to the Royal Docks, August 1949.

Dredging at the entrance to KGV in 1976, PLA grab barge *Albert* loads into hopper barge *Cyril Kirkpatrick* (1964, 847grt).

A closer view of the grab crane at work.

PLA hopper barge *Cyril Kirkpatrick* at Tilbury, 1981. A sister vessel was the *Asa Binns* (1965, 847grt).

PLA tug *Lord Waverley* (1960, 130grt). The PLA took three tugs, *Lord Devonport*, *Lord Waverley* and *Lord Ritchie* in 1959/60 from the yard of James Pollock Sons & Co. at Faversham. These were allocated to the dredging fleet. *Lord Ritchie* was sold in 1977 but the other pair lasted to c. 1992. *Lord Waverley* is seen in 1976.

PLA pusher tug *Broodbank* (1966, 189grt) in 1978. Built by James W. Cook (Wivenhoe) Ltd. for the dredging fleet, she had a length of just 56ft but a width of 31ft. She was sold to Briggs Marine Contracts, Burntisland in 1994 and rebuilt as the *Forth Constructor*.

PLA recovery craft *Yantlet,* 1979.

PLA recovery craft *Hookness,* 1977.

A bow view of *Hookness* at Tilbury in 1980.

Port Health Authority launch *Londinium I,* 1981. The Port Health Authority continues to be a function of the City of London Corporation.

Trinity House *Siren* (1960). Built by J. Samuel White, Cowes, this was one of four sister ships built in 1959–63 for maintaining light-houses and navigation buoys. All were withdrawn by the end of the 1980s.

C. Crawley freshwater boat *Aquator* (1951, 234grt) was formerly Bowker & King's *Bagshot*. She was used to supply fresh water to cruise ships while in port.

Floating cranes

In 1962 the PLA had six floating cranes in service. Smallest was the *London Atlas* with a list capacity of 30 tons, then there were the *London Leviathan* and *London Hercules* at 50 tons, *London Titan* and *London Ajax* at 60 tons, and the massive *London Mammoth* which could lift no less than 200 tons. A new crane added at this time was the 60-ton *London Samson*, built by Holland Cranes in the Netherlands. The deck of this was specially strengthened to carry a deck load of 200 tons, and the 58ft 6in wide vessel had a draught of 8ft fully loaded.

Typical of the kind of work handled by the floating cranes was the loading of British-built buses and railway locomotives being exported to Commonwealth countries. For railway locomotives and carriages, a heavy lift beam was employed. This is a large beam suspended at its mid-point from the crane. The load in turn is suspended from the two ends of the beam.

The PLA also used its floating cranes in other ways. Maintenance and enhancements to the docks were ongoing tasks. The cranes would be used to remove and replace lock gates, for instance, or to erect and reposition quay cranes. In 1957 the lock gates at the entrance to St Katherine's Dock were replaced. The new gates were fabricated at a site in West India Docks, then lifted and transported on the deck of *London Mammoth*, which then installed each of the gates in place. Each gate weighed around 60 tons.

Surely the heaviest lift job ever carried out by floating cranes on the Thames was the lifting into place of the gates for the £435m Thames Barrier in 1981–2. The ten 61-metre long gates weighed around 1,500 tons each, while the separate gate ends weighed 1,200 tons. Two giant floating cranes, each of 800-ton capacity, were hired from the German company Neptun of Hamburg and worked in tandem on the precision lifts. The gate sections were transported to the site on 6,000 ton capacity barges. The barrier was completed in 1982.

The smaller *London Atlas* with a 30-ton lift was more capable of operating in the confined areas of the smaller enclosed docks. It was seen passing along Gallions Reach, Woolwich in 1976.

London Leviathan heads upriver in Gallions Reach.

London Samson operating at the entrance to King George V Dock in June 1977, where it was involved in repairs to the lock gates.

London Mammoth seen in the 1950s, the largest of the floating cranes, with a lifting capacity of 200 tons. After withdrawal it was sold to new owners in Greece but capsized and sank in the Channel while being towed to its new home.

On 11 September 1988 the preserved LNER A3 'Pacific' No. 4472 *Flying Scotsman* is swung aboard the *New Zealand Pacific* at Tilbury Docks by *London Mammoth* for its voyage to Australia, where it arrived on 15 October at Sydney. The engine returned to Tilbury fifteen months later, being offloaded from *La Perouse* on 14 December 1989. *Photo by Geoff Silcock.*

Opposite: One of the giant floating cranes hired from Neptun of Hamburg for the construction of the Thames Barrier is towed upriver at Tilbury by the Bugsier Reederei ocean-going tug *Ajax*. Note how much simpler modern crane design is compared to the 1930s-built *London Mammoth*.

PASSENGER SHIPPING

Passenger/Cruise ships

Passenger liner and later cruise traffic was centred on Tilbury, using the Tilbury Landing Stage as it was known, until 1989. Many of the ships in the 1970s–80s were Russian owned, operated by CTC Cruise Lines who were the UK agents for The Black Sea Shipping Company (BLASCO).

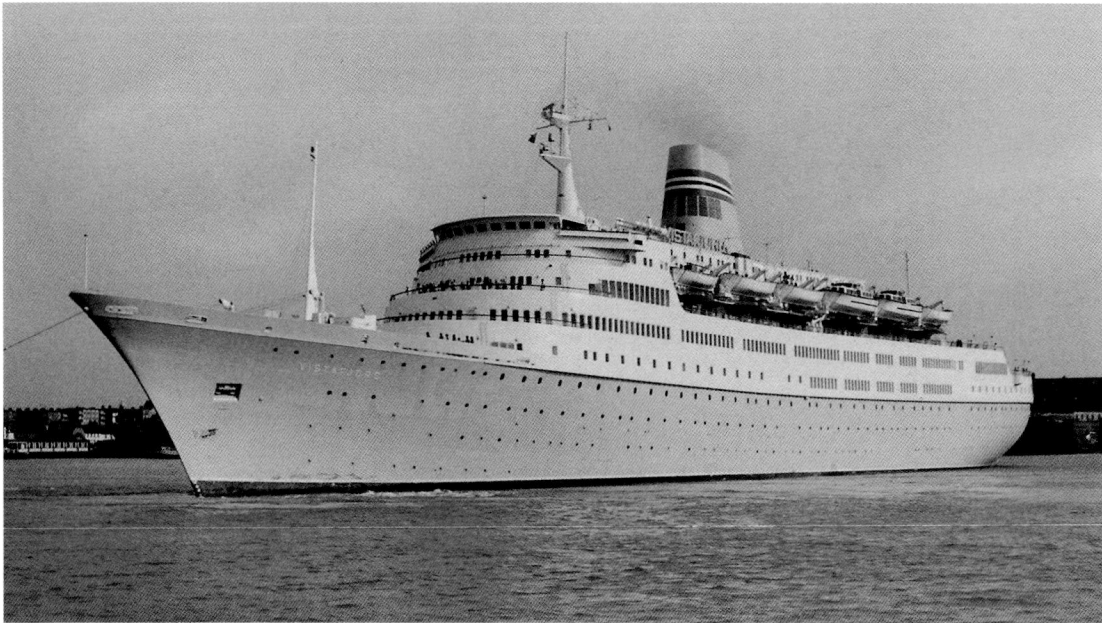

Norwegian America Line *Vistafjord* (1973, 24,292grt), 1980. She later passed to Saga Cruises where she remained in service until 2014.

Norwegian America Line *Sagafjord* (1965, 24,002grt), 1978. Built in France, she ended her career with Saga Cruises as the *Saga Rose*.

Uganda. Built for the British India Line in 1953 and converted as an educational cruise ship in 1967 with provision for 920 students. She transferred to P&O in 1972. She was requisitioned for use as a hospital ship during the Falklands War and 730 casualties were treated aboard her. She was withdrawn in 1985. Seen here in 1980.

Royal Cruise Line *Royal Odyssey* (1964, 17,884grt) made a series of cruises from Tilbury to Baltic ports between 1981 and 1987. Taken in 1982.

Fred Olsen & Co. *Black Watch* (1966, 9,499grt). Along with *Black Prince* these were built as passenger/car ferries then converted for cruising in 1986–7. In winter months they sailed from Tilbury to the Canary Islands bringing back fruit and tomatoes to Millwall Docks.

Russian owned *Baltika* (1939, 7,494grt) seen on the landing stage. She was named *Vyacheslav Molotov* until 1957, normally running a Leningrad–Helsinki–London service. Later used for cruising, withdrawal came in 1987. Seen in 1982.

Fedor Shalyapin in 1981. Originally Cunard Line's *Ivernia* (1955, 21,406grt). In 1962 she was converted to become cruise ship *Franconia* and was sold to Russia in 1973.

The *Mikhail Kalinin* (1958, 4,871grt) departs from Tilbury landing stage. Note the hammer and sickle emblem on the funnel, found on most Russian shipping at the time. These ships were operated by the London-based CTC Lines (later CTC Cruise Lines). 1980.

Mikhail Lermontov (1972, 19,872grt) was the fifth and last of the *Ivan Franko* class. She met an untimely end in 1986, sinking after hitting underwater rocks off New Zealand. Sister ship, the former *Alexandr Pushkin* (1965, 19860grt) was still a regular at Tilbury in 2019 as the *Marco Polo* with Cruise & Maritime Voyages (CMV).

Here seen in 1979. Polish Ocean Lines owned cruise ship *Stefan Batory* (1952, 15,244 grt). Previously named *Maasdam* until 1966, she was built for the Holland America Line along with her sister ship *Rijndam*. They were originally intended to be cargo/passenger liners, being altered while under construction to carry c.850 tourist and 39 first-class passengers. Polish Ocean Lines bought her in 1968 and used her on cruises and a Poland–UK–Canada service. She last visited Tilbury in 1987, soon afterwards being sold to become an accommodation ship for the Swedish immigration authorities.

This is the *Odessa* (1974, 13,758grt) in 1982.

Kareliya (1976, 15,065grt) operated for CTC Cruise Lines from 1981 to 1994. Note the stern door, a legacy from her original use as a Black Sea cruise ferry. From 1982–9 she sailed under the name *Leonid Brezhnev*.

Ferries

All change at Woolwich

The 5 October 2018 marked the end of a local era, for that was when the Woolwich ferries that I have known for much of my life ran for the last time.

The Woolwich Free Ferry dates back to 1884 when the Metropolitan Board of Works proposed a free passenger and vehicle ferry between the north and south banks of the River Thames at Woolwich. There was already a passenger ferry service here – indeed there had been a ferry crossing here for hundreds of years. The coming of the railway age saw the first railway in London linking London with Greenwich. But Parliament would not allow the extension of the railway on to the important town of Woolwich with its army garrison and Arsenal. This was because the railway would have to tunnel under Maze Hill and they were concerned that this work might upset the workings of Greenwich Observatory from which Greenwich Mean Time was set, which was adopted by the Railway Clearing House in 1847 to become standard railway time. So the Eastern Counties & Thames Junction Railway saw an opportunity and built a rail line from Stratford to North Woolwich on the opposite bank. They then commenced their own ferry service across the river.

By the time the free ferry started in March 1889, the Metropolitan Board of Works had been replaced by the London County Council, who continued to maintain the service. This killed off the railway's ferry which ceased on 1 October 1908. In October 1912 a foot tunnel was built under the river to supplement the ferry or provide pedestrian access when the ferry was not running. By now there were the extensive Royal Docks and numerous industries on the north bank, including rubber, soap and the sugar refineries of Henry Tate and Abram Lyle, opened in 1878 and 1883. These later merged as Tate & Lyle in 1921 and both refinery buildings remain in use to this day.

The original ferries were replaced by four new steam paddle ferries. *Squires* and *Gordon* were built at Cowes in 1922–3 and *John Benn* and *Will Crooks* in 1930. These impressive vessels measured 166ft x 44ft. They could carry 1,000 passengers and up to 100 tons of vehicles. Their paddles were independently driven to maximise manoeuvrability. The boilers of the two separate engines burnt coke produced at the nearby Beckton gas works.

The steam ferries lasted until 1963 when they were replaced by three diesel vessels built by the Caledon Shipbuilding & Engineering Company, Dundee. These had two Voith Schneider propulsion units each, one at each end. They could carry 200 tons of vehicles but only some 500 passengers. They were named after prominent local politicians, *Ernest Bevin, John Burns* and *James Newman*. At first these continued to use the old loading link span piers and so were side loading like their predecessors. But in 1966 new piers were opened which allowed for the more convenient end loading 'drive on – drive off' procedure.

The London County Council was replaced by the Greater London Council in 1965. When this was abolished by Margaret Thatcher in 1985 the ferry management became the responsibility of the London Borough of Greenwich (now the Royal Borough of Greenwich), latterly on behalf of Transport for London (TfL). But their involvement ended in 2008, and after a period when it was run by Serco, Briggs Marine now operate the ferry on behalf of TfL.

Although with the closure of the Royal Docks in 1983, the number of passengers using the ferries and tunnel has declined, although the ferry remains important as one of the few vehicle crossing points in east London. Because of the need to maintain height for navigation, there were no bridges east of Tower Bridge until the Queen Elizabeth II Dartford bridge opened to supplement the tunnel there in 1991, and these remain as the only bridges. There are two Thames road tunnels in east London. Rotherhithe tunnel, built in 1908 is narrow and twisting and now has a width and height restriction of 6ft 6in so is only accessible to cars. The other is the Blackwall tunnel which gets heavily congested. A proposal for a bridge east of Woolwich was rejected over environmental concerns that it would lead to the destruction of the ancient Abbey Wood. A new road tunnel has been approved at Silvertown but work is yet to start, and there are major concerns these days over air quality and traffic emissions in London, so this may not happen.

Meanwhile the ferries carried on in daily service, carrying cars and lorries, and a few passengers. They can take vehicles up to 15ft high that are too tall for the tunnels. Although no bus route has ever been scheduled to cross by the ferry, double-deck buses sometimes use it when being transferred between garages north and south, as the Blackwall tunnel can only accommodate single-deck vehicles. However most passengers now use the Docklands Light Railway (DLR), which since 2009 has run from Stratford to Woolwich Arsenal via London City Airport. This replaced the former railway line from Stratford to North Woolwich which had latterly formed part of the North London Line, with electric trains running through to Richmond. This closed in December 2006. Part of the track bed is now used by the DLR while another section has been incorporated into Crossrail, which will provide another crossing to Woolwich before terminating at Abbey Wood. The first stage of this was due to open in December 2018 but has now been put back to at least 2021.

Normally two ferries were used on weekdays, with one at weekends. But after 55 years they were considered life-expired and so two new vessels were ordered in 2016 to replace them. These have been built by Polish company Remontowa and are diesel-electric hybrid vessels. As well as carrying cars and lorries, they have dedicated space for cyclists and can carry 150 passengers. The old ferries were quickly towed away to Le Havre in France for scrapping. However, the new ferries did not enter service straight away as work needed to be done on modifying the piers before they started in February 2019. The new vessels are named *Ben Woollicott* (a 19-year old deckhand who drowned after being dragged overboard in 2011) and *Dame Vera Lynn*.

Steam paddle ferry *Will Crooks* (1930, 621grt). There are many passengers but no vehicles visible in this view from the late 1940s.

New Woolwich Ferry *Ernest Bevin, 1960s.*

Woolwich Ferry *James Newman* in the 1960s with the power station.

A car boards at the south Woolwich ferry linkspan, 1975.

Ernest Bevin, now with GLC promotional lettering.

Tilbury–Gravesend ferry

A ferry crossing between Gravesend and Tilbury has existed since medieval times and is mentioned in the Domesday Book. Gravesend Corporation ran a ferry for which they built the Town Pier in 1834. In 1854 the London, Tilbury & Southend Railway reached Tilbury and commenced their own ferry service in 1862, later taking over the Corporation service and Town Pier in 1864. The service in due course passed to British Railway's

Tilbury Ferry *Edith* (1961, 214grt) in 1976.

Sealink subsidiary. Four steam ferries built by A. W. Roberts & Co, the *Catherine, Edith, Gertrude* and *Rose* ran until 1961 when they were replaced by three diesel craft built by J. S. White & Sons of Cowes, the *Catherine, Edith* and *Rose*. Two steam vehicle ferries, the *Tessa* (1924) and *Mimie* (1926) could carry 20–30 cars each. These were withdrawn on 31 December 1964 following the opening of the Dartford tunnel. Passenger numbers declined as well once the tunnel was available, so in 1967 the *Rose* was transferred to Caledonian MacBrayne in Scotland, becoming the *Keppel* on the Largs–Millport run. Sealink was sold off in 1984 and sold on in 1990 to Stena Line. Since then the ferry service has had a number of different owners and vessels.

Edith again in 1977.

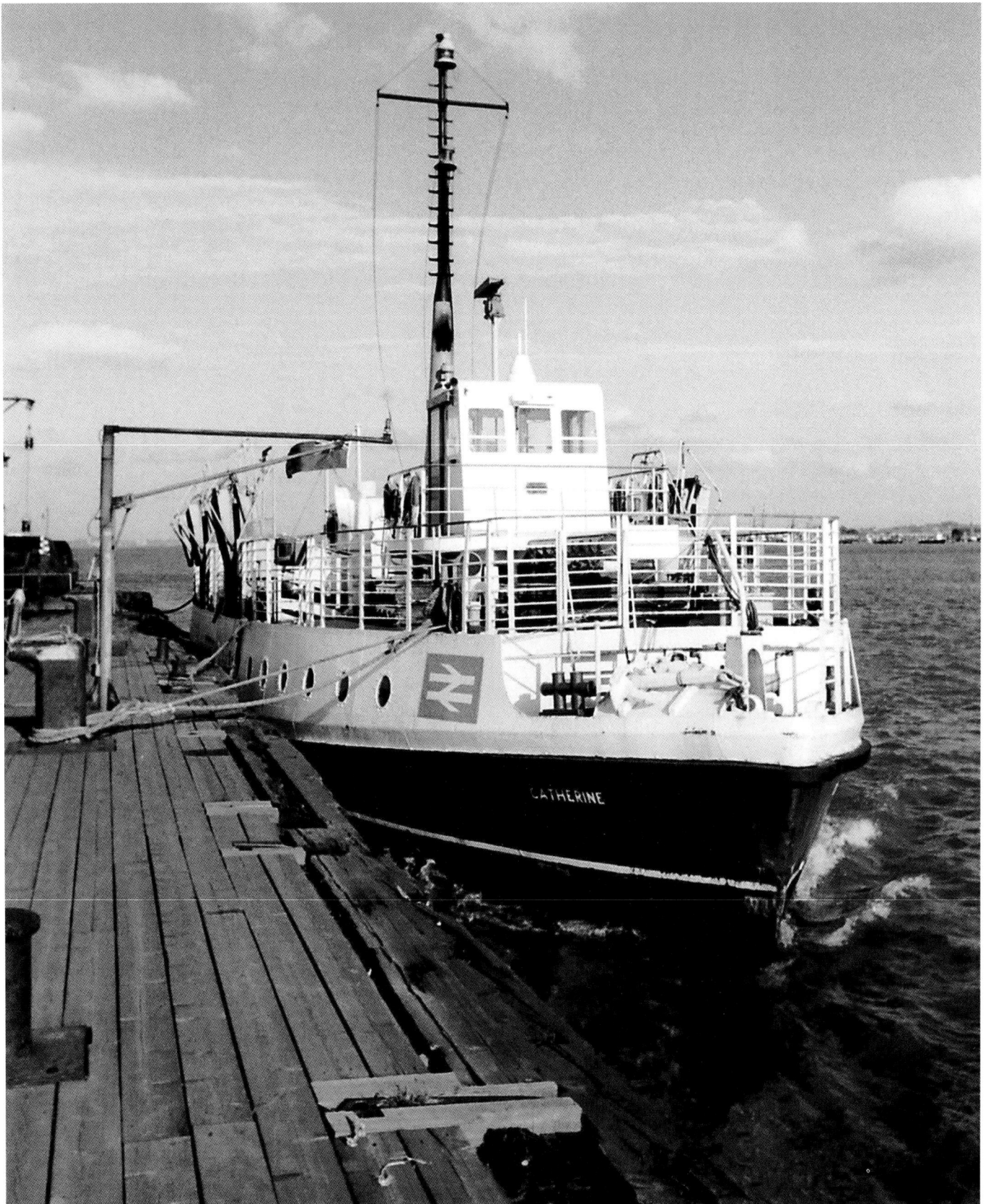

Catherine at the Tilbury Landing Stage, 1977.

You can't please them all! A reminder that unlike Woolwich, the Tilbury Ferry was not a free service. 1980.

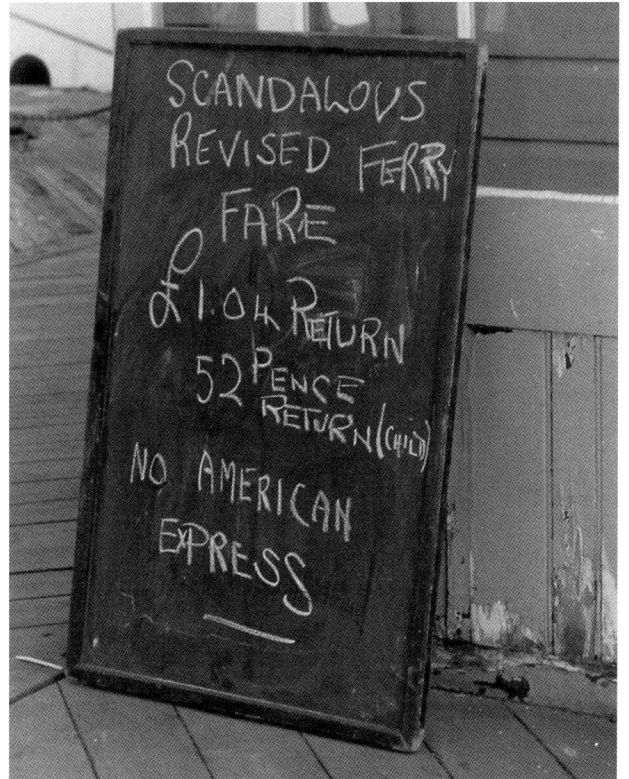

In October 1977 Sealink trialled the use of the small (1957,35grt) *Humphrey Gilbert* on the Tilbury–Gravesend ferry service. This proved a fiasco when the base of her life raft collapsed on deck after a few bumps against the landing stage. *Humphrey Gilbert* was one of a pair that had built for the River Dart crossing between Kingswear and Dartmouth. Here she is seen laid up at Greenwich on 8 October. *Photo by Malcolm Batten.*

Other ferry services

A P&O Jetfoil service from London to Zeebrugge, Belgium, started in June 1977, departing from St Katherine Pier by Tower Bridge. This was withdrawn in September 1980 due to lack of support. Shown in 1978.

P&O Boeing Jetfoil *Jetferry 2* at speed passing Gravesend on its inward journey to London, 1980. The Jetfoils could reach speeds of 40 knots.

London Hoverservices ran hovercraft from Tower Pier between July 1973 and October 1974. Then Speed Hydrofoils took over the service with leased Russian-built hydrofoil *Raketa Greenwich*. This is seen having just passed under Waterloo Bridge on 30 November 1974. Floating debris causing damage to the foils led to poor timekeeping, and an end to the experiment came in September 1976. *Photo by Malcolm Batten.*

Pleasure craft

Pleasure craft offered (and indeed still offer) trips for Londoners and tourists alike along the Thames from Tower Pier or Charing Cross, downriver to Greenwich or upriver towards Hampton Court. Improvements to marine diesel design, the result of wartime experience, made diesel power more economic than steam for such craft, and most steamers were converted between 1945–50. The last to be steam powered was the *Ferry Prince*. This was a former Portsmouth–Gosport ferry, built in 1939 and acquired by Thames Pleasurecraft in 1966. She ran for a while under steam but was converted before the 1967 season. The similar *Ferry Princess* was also bought but had already been converted.

For many of the industrial workers and office staff of London, an affordable holiday might have featured a day trip by excursion steamer to the seaside. The first such services were inaugurated by the Woolwich Steam Packet Co. as long ago as 1834, departing from Charing Cross pier. By 1893 there were regular seasonal services to Southend, Clacton, Felixstowe and Great Yarmouth. These excursions proved very popular, the trip down the Thames past what was then the world's greatest port all adding to the interest. Not even the worst disaster on the river, in 1878, when the PS *Princess Alice* collided with a collier at Gallions Reach, Woolwich, and sank with the loss of some 700 lives could deter Londoners.

During the Second World War, the paddle steamers were requisitioned as mine-sweepers, hospital ships or troop carriers. Several saw action at Dunkirk, such as the *Royal Daffodil* rescuing hundreds of soldiers. Others were less lucky – *Queen of the Channel* and *Crested Eagle* were both sunk during the evacuation. A number of piers were also damaged, but in 1948, General Steam Navigation Co., the main operating company, resumed services with five ships. Services ran to Clacton and Herne Bay, but mines off the Kent coast prevented stops at Margate. A new diesel screw-driven craft *Royal Sovereign* was also delivered in 1948, a sign of confidence in the future.

Business thrived for a while. The *Royal Sovereign* was sailing regularly from Gravesend and Southend to Boulogne and back in a day. But then, in the late 1950s when we 'never had it so good', standards of living and car ownership rose dramatically. More people were going abroad on holiday and the paddle steamers seemed dated and rapidly lost their glamour. For the 1966 season the GSNC only ran at weekends,

using the two diesel screw-driven vessels the *Royal Sovereign* and *Queen of the Channel*. At the beginning of December the service was withdrawn altogether. The last regular paddle steamer to operate had been the New Medway Steam Packet Company's *Medway Queen*, built in 1924 and withdrawn in 1963. She was later acquired for preservation by the Medway Queen Preservation Society and restoration work continues at Gillingham. In 1966/7 the Clyde paddle steamer *Jennie Deans* came to London as the *Queen of the South* but she was plagued by boiler problems and was scrapped at the end of 1967.

After this the opportunity for Londoners to travel down the Thames to the seaside would be lost until the former River Clyde paddle steamer PS *Waverley*, now in the hands of the Paddle Steamer Preservation Society, began to make an annual fortnight of sailings on the Thames from 1978 onwards, which she has continued to do most years since then.

General Steam Navigation Co. Ltd *Royal Sovereign* was built in 1948 to replace paddle steamers lost during the war whilst requisitioned for use as minesweepers. She is seen here passing Woolwich in September 1950. GSNC operations ceased in December 1966 and she was sold in 1967.

P&A Campbell owned the *Devonia* (1956, 921 grt) seen in 1977. She was a former Scilly Islands ferry named *Scillonian* until 1977.

Vessels at Lambeth pier in the 1960s.

A well patronised upriver pleasure steamer, the *Princess Beatrice*, about to enter the lock at Teddington. Originally built in 1896 she was owned by Joseph Mears Motors & Launches Ltd from 1914–46, then Thames Launches Ltd from 1947 until 1963. Originally a single-screw steamer she was converted to diesel c.1955.

COURTESY VISITS

Naval visitors

Australian Navy destroyer D41 *Brisbane*. She was built in the USA by the Defoe Shipbuilding Co., Bay City, Michigan in 1966. Seen at Tilbury, 1977.

Norwegian Navy corvette F310 *Sleipner* launched in 1963. Seen in 1977.

UK Navy M1173 *Mersey* (1957) ex *Pollington,* seen in 1981.

TA31 heads back out to sea after a courtesy visit and is passing Woolwich in 1977.

Taken in 1982, *Sir Lamorak* (1972) was a Ro-Ro ship on charter to the Ministry of Defence. Owned by Cenargo Ltd she had carried various previous names. The charter ended in 1986 after which she became the *Merchant Trader*.

Other visitors

Royal Yacht *Britannia* moored in the Upper Pool by Tower Pier 1977. Retired in 1997, she is now a tourist attraction at Leith.

Sally Viking Line Ro-Ro car ferry *The Viking* (1974, 5,286grt). This was ex *Viking 5* in 1981.

Townsend Thoresen car ferry *Free Enterprise II* (1965, 4,122grt), 1979.

Catamaran ferry *Highland Seabird* passing Woolwich. Owned by Western Ferries and registered at Glasgow, she had been acting as a demonstrator. In May 1982 she had been trialled by Merseyside PTE on the River Mersey ferry services.

Ben Line drilling ship *Ben Ocean Lancer* (10,823grt) was a visitor when new in 1977.

Also visiting when new in 1981 was Geest Line's *Geestbay* (1981, 7,730grt). Taken passing Tilbury, she was bound for the Upper Pool on a publicity visit. As well as her main cargo of bananas, like others in the Geest fleet she had accommodation for twelve first-class passengers.

SAIL TRAINING SHIPS

The *Amerigo Vespucci* (1931, 3,543grt) was a sail training ship with the Italian Navy.

The smaller *Christian Bach* seen in 1979 was built in Denmark in 1953.

HERITAGE SHIPPING

Thames barges

While barges were declining as a commercial proposition, interest in them was growing for other uses. The idea of barges for holiday cruising developed after the Thames Barge Sailing Club was founded in 1948. After initially chartering, they then bought *Arrow*. Under the guidance of a professional skipper, members could sail her from a base on the Medway to London and back. The club bought the motorised *Pudge* in 1968 and re-rigged her. They also owned the *Centaur*.

In 1952 John Kemp had the idea of preserving a trading sailing barge and founded the Thames Sailing Barge Trust, later renamed the Sailing Barge Preservation Society. The society bought *Medway* from Horlocks in 1956 and worked her in trade until 1959. The society was wound up in 1959 but *Memory* continued to work as an 'outward bound' type cruise ship.

The East Coast Sail Trust was founded in 1971 by Hervey Benham and John Kemp. They owned the *Thalatta*, which provided educational and adventure holidays for children. Chartering for cruising on a commercial basis grew in the 1960s. In 1964 the Maldon Yacht and Barge Charter Co. Ltd were using *Memory* and *Kitty* on such work. Maldon has become quite a centre for such enterprise since then.

Companies also began to use and acquire barges for promotional work and entertaining clients. Bell's Whisky bought *Hydrogen* for such work after chartering Crescent Shipping's *Sirdar*. In 1964 Tate & Lyle, the sugar refiners at Silvertown, bought *May* with four purposes in mind: preservation, sail training experience for apprentices, to continue her in trade, and for chartering, publicity work etc. Since then she sailed extensively, including carrying cargo such as 50 tonnes of stone from Portland for the restoration of St Paul's Cathedral in 1972. She was registered for 50 tons of cargo and 46 passengers on the Thames and Medway. She is now in private ownership. *Will Everard* was sold to a private buyer in 1967 on condition that her name was shortened to just *Will*. In 1977 she was bought by OCL and passed on takeover to P&O.

She was sold in 1999 and has had several owners since. *Cabby* was retained by Crescent Shipping, successors to London & Rochester Trading Co.

Taylor Woodrow, developers of St Katharine Dock, bought *Lady Daphne* as an exhibit there and for promotional work.

In 1978 the Sailing Barge Association was set up to represent owners, while in 1981 the Association of Bargemen was established to represent enthusiasts and volunteer crewmen.

With the decline in working barges came a decline in the yards that built and repaired them. Cook's yard at Maldon survives and is a centre for restoration as well as cruising. The Dolphin Sailing Barge Museum Trust at Sittingbourne has restored a yard there to a working museum where a number of barges including *Oak* and *Glenway* have been restored.

At the end of the 1980s there were around seventy Thames barges known to be still in existence, of which more than thirty were in active sailing order. At any one time several barges can be found berthed in St Katharine Dock. Regulars there have included *Lady Daphne*, *Beric*, *Ardwina*, *Edith May* and *Raybel*. During the summer months most of these and others will be active. The barge races, started in 1863, which encouraged the type's refinement continued except for the war years until 1963. Since then there have been regular events each year attended by private and company owned craft. These take place in a number of places including Gravesend and Southend.

In May 2011, former 'stackie' barge *Dawn* carried a cargo of hay, loaded I believe on the River Blackwater, down to London and into St Katharine Dock for a TV programme about old trade routes. In July 2020 the same vessel was used in conjunction with the 1916 built gaff schooner *De Gallant* which had brought a cargo of food and wine to London's St Katharine Dock in an environmentally conscious and sustainable way. *De Gallant* then sailed to Queenborough on the Isle of Sheppey where *Dawn* took some of the cargo onwards to Thames estuary towns.

Lady Daphne (1923, 117grt) under sail in 1976.

Ironsides in 1979. As the name implies, she has an iron hull.

Hoseasons restored barge *Xylonite* seen passing Gravesend in 1979.

Sugar refiners Tate & Lyle acquired the barge *May* in 1964. Here she is seen passing Tilbury on a trip to Ipswich in 1982.

Others

When St Katharine Dock closed some of the listed warehouses were converted to offices as the World Trade Centre, while others were demolished to make way for a hotel. The dock itself was redeveloped as a marina. The Maritime Trust, founded in 1969, had acquired a number of historic craft and were invited to display some of their collection. The Trust's collection was dispersed after 1986 but the marina remains a regular haven for many of the Thames sailing barges and other preserved craft.

Tug *Challenge*, 212 tons gross was built in 1931 by Alexander Hall & Co., Aberdeen, for the Elliot Steam Tug Co, Gravesend. When withdrawn in 1972 she was the last steam driven ship-handling tug on the Thames. She was sold to Taylor Woodrow for preservation in 1973 and was kept initially in St Katharine Dock marina as seen here in June 1979. In the background is the Dickens Inn pub.

Tug *Portwey* at St Katharine Dock. She was owned by the Falmouth Docks & Engineering Co. Ltd and was built in 1927. She was sold for preservation in 1967 and donated to the Maritime Trust in 1982. Behind can just be seen the bows of *Discovery* (before she moved to Dundee), 1983.

Lightship *Nore* at St Katharine Dock in 1979. Built in 1931 this was one of the craft preserved by the Maritime Trust.

Also owned by the Maritime Trust and on display at the dock in 1979 was the steam-powered herring drifter *Lydia Eva*.

The former Admiralty steam tug *Torque* was berthed alongside the site of the former Harland & Wolff shipyard at North Woolwich whilst an attempt was made to restore her. August 1979.

HMS *Belfast* built in 1938 came to the Upper Pool for preservation in 1971. Seen here in 1977, with motor torpedo boat *M1216* alongside on a courtesy visit. Note the derelict former warehouses behind – the area has since been redeveloped.

After the General Steam Navigation Co. withdrawal at the end of the 1966 season, there had been little chance for passengers to travel downriver beyond Greenwich. However, the *Waverley* began making seasonal sailings on the Thames from 1978 and has continued to do so most years since then. Here she leaves Tower Pier on 29 April 1978 with a healthy load of passengers. *Photo by Malcolm Batten.*

When the River Humber ferries were replaced by the new Humber bridge, the last three steam paddle ferries in the BR Sealink fleet were withdrawn. The *Wingfield Castle* (1934, 556grt) was laid up initially at the entrance to the Royal docks at North Woolwich in 1975 before transfer to Swansea for conversion to a restaurant ship. This did not happen, and she was eventually preserved at Hartlepool where she was built.

Another of the Humber ferries, the *Tattershall Castle* (1934) was withdrawn in 1972 and also came to the Thames, but has remained. She has been a floating pub/restaurant moored by Hungerford Bridge since 1975, initially looking like this as seen in 1976. Unfortunately, a refit at Yarmouth in 2003–4 saw her lose many of her original features, including the bridge superstructure and paddle wheels.

Former River Clyde paddle steamer *Caledonia* was built in 1934 for the London, Midland & Scottish Railway. Withdrawn in 1969, she was bought by Bass Charington and was converted to a pub/restaurant named *Old Caledonia*, moored close to Waterloo Bridge. Unfortunately, she was destroyed by fire on 27 April 1980 and was later towed away for scrap. Her steam engines survive at the Hollycombe Steam Museum near Liphook.

Old Caledonia makes her final journey down river to the scrapyard in 1980, being towed past Tilbury Fort.

POSTSCRIPT – RUNDOWN AND RENAISSANCE

Most of the ships seen in this book are no more. Some of the locations have changed dramatically, as the London docks were closed and redeveloped. The Royal Docks, the last in the London area, closed to general traffic in 1983 and were then just used for laid-up shipping until final closure in 1985 for redevelopment. The Port of London is still thriving and the PLA still has a responsibility for maintaining the river, pilotage etc, although it no longer owns the docks. Tilbury Docks were privatised by a management buy-out in February 1992 and sold on to Forth Ports in 1996 for £131.6m.

From November 2013 the new £1.5 billion DP World London Gateway container terminal has opened at Thameshaven on the site of the former Shell Haven oil refinery. This 1,500 acre site has been developed in stages with berths and a logistics park. Now it can take three maximum size ships at a time. The existing roads and rail line to the refinery have been upgraded to provide excellent access facilities for the surge in container traffic. As a consequence, Northfleet Hope has lost many of the larger companies and ships to the Gateway and now mainly sees smaller feeder ships.

The opening of the M25 Motorway and the Queen Elizabeth II bridge at Dartford led to new private wharves being established nearby with easy access to the motorway. This was particularly pertinent for Ro-Ro traffic and so Purfleet Deep Wharf, now used by Cobelfret Ferries, and the Thames Euro terminal, formerly used by Dart Ferries, were built. This marked a shift in Ro-Ro traffic from Scandinavian forest products (which still continues) to lorry trailer traffic to/from Europe as originally introduced by the Atlantic Steam Navigation Company.

Other private wharves such as that of Seacon on the Isle of Dogs have also relocated to the Tilbury area. However there are still oil storage terminals such as Vopak at Purfleet and aggregates terminals such as Angerstein Wharf at Charlton. Bulk carriers still come to Tate & Lyle's refinery.

The Woolwich and Tilbury ferries both still run, albeit with different craft and operators. Pleasure craft for tourist traffic still run between Tower Pier and Greenwich all year round. A new venture developed since 1999 has become Thames Clippers, offering fast frequent commuter services from Woolwich in the east through central London and to Putney in the west.

Bulk Carrier *Matilde R* (1966, 26,634grt) ex *Matilde* in 1982 plus others laid up in KGV. Behind her is the *Portofino* (1966, 27,721grt) ex *Har Meron* in 1974. Both were owned by the Maritime Overseas Corporation, USA.

A later view of laid up shipping in KGV. The *Matilde R* seems to have gone but alongside the *Portofino* is the *Continental Pioneer* (1969, 15,474) from the same company. A barrier of lighters prevents any other craft from entering or leaving. Partly visible just behind these Greek bulk carrier *Ephistos*, which was later destined to become the last laid up ship to leave the Royals.

Harland & Wolff's ship repair works was by the entrance to King George V Dock. Here the buildings are being demolished by a crane wielding a ball and chain in 1978. The site remained vacant for many years, until the construction of luxury flats started in 1999. With the changes to cargo handling and closure of the docks came the end of many ancillary services such as ship and lighter repair, export packers and ship chandlers.

A Harland & Wolff advert from the PLA directory 1963. The works closed in 1972.

The Upper Pool no longer sees commercial shipping, and the only traffic that ventures beyond London Bridge these days tends to be either containerised domestic refuse or building materials for riverside developments. Cory Environmental have the contract for the containerised rubbish, and tug *Redoubt* is one of four new tugs delivered in 2010 for this purpose. HMS *Belfast* remains moored in the Upper Pool as a visitor attraction, owned by the Imperial War Museum since 1978, now repainted in North Atlantic camouflage livery since 1993. Cruise ships and vessels on courtesy visits moor alongside it on occasions. Tower Bridge now is only opened for shipping a few times a week. Hays Wharf has become the Hays Galleria shopping arcade – seen behind the 'kids go free' notice. 2014. *Photo by Malcolm Batten.*

This old cast iron 'Gents' stood outside the Board of Trade offices at Custom House. Here on 28 January 1979 it was adorned with posters from groups campaigning against the closure of the docks. *Photo by Malcolm Batten.*

The skyline at West India Dock has changed dramatically as the area has been redeveloped as the Docklands financial district. A few cranes have been cosmetically left in place at the lock entrance. The lock is operational as vessels frequently call in on courtesy visits – mainly naval craft or sail training ships. Just visible on the left is the red and black funnel of the preserved steam tug *Portwey*, which is now kept in the dock. February 2020. *Photo by Malcolm Batten.*

Looking west from the lock entrance to King George V Dock in 2019. The strip between this and the Royal Albert Dock is the runway of London City Airport from which a plane has just taken off. In the distance are the towers of Canary Wharf and the Docklands development. Again, the lock is operational with a new electrically powered bridge, and shipping can pass through to the Royal Victoria Dock and the Excel Exhibition Centre on certain occasions. *Photo by Malcolm Batten.*

Grain-handling facilities were transferred from the Royal Docks to the new Tilbury Grain Terminal in 1969. But a reminder of the past can still be seen in the form of the derelict Spillers Millennium Mills at the Royal Docks. Seen here from the Docklands Light Railway in 2018. *Photo by Malcolm Batten.*

The new London Gateway Port in 2018. This opened in stages from 2013 and can handle up to three of the largest container ships at a time. United Arab Shipping Company *UASC Al Khor* was on the berth in October 2018 when photographed from on board the *Waverley. Photo by Malcolm Batten.*